To my Sister in memory
of our Mother –
P. 102 –
love always Bobbie 2010

قصص من أمهاتنا
[لقاء بين النساء من بريطانيا وفلسطين]

Stories from our Mothers
(meetings of British and Palestinian women)

هذا المشروع بتنظيم من جمعية صداقة كامدن أبوديس ودار الصداقة فى أبوديس، وقد تضمن زيارتان رائعتان للنساء فى كلا الاتجاهان، فى تشرين ثانى 2009 زارت مجموعة من النساء البريطانيات فلسطين وفى آذار 2010 زارت مجموعة من النساء الفلسطينيات بريطانيا.

This project, organised by Camden Abu Dis Friendship Association and Dar Assadaqa, Abu Dis, included two wonderful women's exchanges. Women from Britain visited Palestine in November 2009 and women from Palestine visited Britain in May 2010.

احدى الزائرات البريطانيات عملت على انتاج فيلم عن الزيارات والفيلم متوفر الان عند جمعية صداقة كامدن أبوديس، هناك معلومات أكثر عن المشروع على www.camdenabudis,net/stories.html

One of the visitors from Britain has made a film of the visits which is available from Camden Abu Dis Friendship Association. There is more information on the project at **www.camdenabudis,net/stories.html**

تم تمويل المشروع بشكل جزئى من مؤسسة آنا ليندا

The project was part-funded by the Anna Lindh Foundation

نشر الكتاب فى أيلول 2010
جمعية صداقة كامدن أبوديس

Published September 2010 by
Camden Abu Dis Friendship Association (CADFA)

تصميم إيد فيدنبيرج
طبع فى بريطانيا مطبعة لايتن سورس

Designed by Ed Fredenburgh
Printed In Britain by Lightning Source
© CADFA
ISBN 978-0-9556136-3-0
EAN 9780955613630

Previous books that CADFA has published, which can be bought online from Amazon: **www.amazon.co.uk**
or from the CADFA website: **www.camdenabudis.net/shopbooklets.html**
In Palestine, they can be bought from **Dar Assadaqa, Abu Dis**

هذة مجموعة الكتب التى أصدرتها جمعية صداقة كامدن أبوديس. يمكن شرائها على موقع الامازون : **www.amazon.co.uk**
او على موقع جمعية صداقة كامدن أبوديس
www.camdenabudis.net/shopbooklet.html
متوفرة كذلك فى أبوديس دار الصداقة، أبوديس

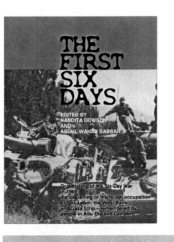

The First Six Days:
An oral history of the Six-Day War in 1967: the beginning of the Israeli occupation of Jerusalem, the West Bank and the Gaza Strip – remembered by people in Abu Dis and Camden
£8

الستة ايام الاولى
رواية شعبية لاحداث ستة ايام من الحرب عام 1967: بداية الاحتلال الاسرائيلى للقدس الشرقية والضفة الغربية وقطاع غزة- من ذاكرة أهالى أبوديس وكامدن.
£8

Voices From Abu Dis:
Abu Dis is an East Jerusalem suburb, now surrounded and cut off by the Israeli Separation Wall, military checkpoints and massively expanding Israeli settlements. These letters and stories sent to friends in Camden show something of what life is like for the people of Abu Dis, sixty years after the Universal Declaration of Human Rights
£10

أصوات من أبوديس
تقع أبوديس فى الجهة الشرقية من القدس، وهى محاطة الان بجدار فاصل ونقاط تفتيش عسكرية ومستوطنات ضخمة ، هذة الرسائل والقصص ارسلت الى الاصداقاء فى كامدن تظهر أشكال الحياة للناس فى أبوديس بعد ستون عاماً من الاعلان العالمى لحقوق الانسان.
£10

For Hammam:
Information for young people looking at the human rights situation in Palestine, based on the work of young people from Palestine and Britain during summer 2009 in the Youth Ambassadors for Human Rights project. Dedicated to Hammam, an Abu Dis teenager shot in the head by an Israeli soldier
£10

الى همام
معلومات للشباب حول قضايا حقوق الانسان فى فلسطين، تم إنتاج هذا العمل بمشاركة مجموعة من الشباب من فلسطين وبريطانيا خلال شهر حزيران من العام 2009 ضمن فعاليات مشروع سفراء شباب من أجل حقوق الانسان. وقد أهدى هذا الكتاب الى همام وهو مراهق من أبوديس أطلق الجنود الإسرائيليون الرصاص على رأسه.
£10

قصـص
مـن
أمــهاتنا

Stories
from our
Mothers

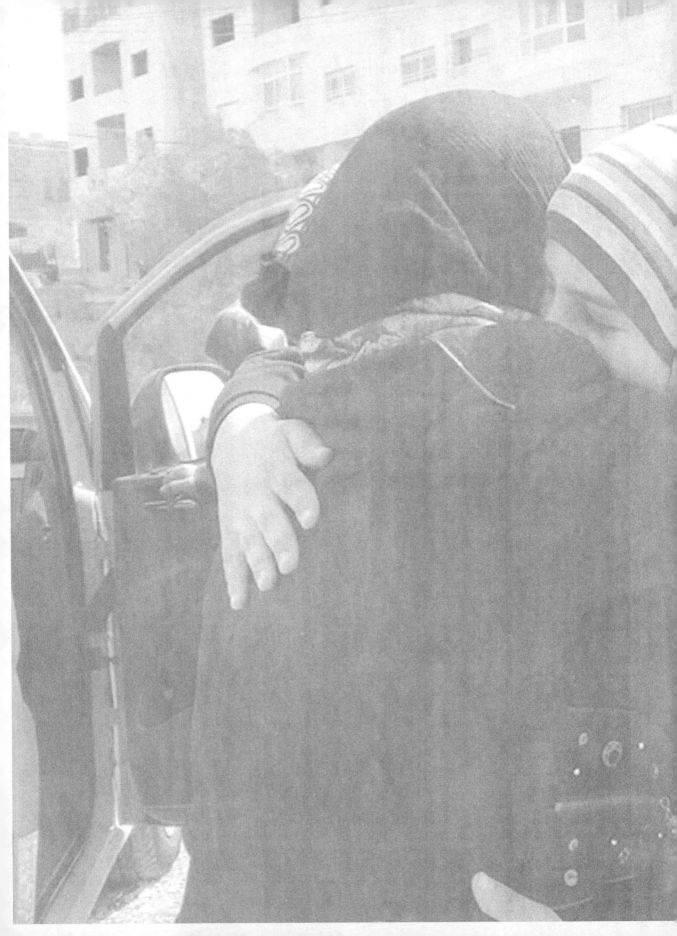

قصص من أمهاتنا

تحرير ننديتا داوسن وعبد الوهاب صباح
EDITED BY NANDITA DOWSON AND
ABDUL WAHAB SABBAH

Stories from our Mothers

Camden Abu Dis Friendship Association
promoting human rights and respect for international humanitarian law
PO Box 34265 London NW5 2WD   Charity number 1112717
0845 458 1167
www.camdenabudis.net
Also on Facebook

إهـداء   Dedication

الى كل بناتنا   **to all of our daughters**

الكتاب مهدى الى النساء من فلسطين وبريطانيا اللواتى
خطون خطوة ايجابية جداً، مصممات على مطالبهن
بالتغيير، آملين بان ينتح عن (قصص من أمهاتنا)
لفلسطين فى المستقبل قصص السعيدة.

This book is dedicated to the Palestinian and British
women who make such a positive, determined demand
for change, hoping a future 'Stories from our Mothers'
that focuses on Palestinian women will be able to
produce happier stories.

ix

المحتويات   Contents

المحتويات   Contents

xi

عرفان

تود جمعية صداقة كامدن ابوديس ودار الصداقة فى ابوديس والتى نظمت تبادل الزيارات وقامت على المشروع فى أن تشكر كل الأفراد والمؤسسات النسويه والمجموعات التى ساعدت فى انجاز هذا المشروع. لقد كان هناك العديد من المؤسسات التى شاركت فى إنجاح مشروع قصص من أمهاتنا: الرجاء مشاهدة القائمة فى صفحة 148-9.

هناك الكثير الكثير ممن ساعدوا ولكن نخص بالذكر مركز دراسات الجندر فى جامعة القدس فى ابوديس فلسطين ومركز دراسات الجندر فى جامعة سواس فى كامدن حيث تم عقد ورشات العمل الخاصة بالمشروع فى هذين المركزين وتم طرح العديد من القصص الموجودة فى الكتاب.

الشكر الجزيل لمؤسسة آنا ليند للدور المهم الذى لعبته ليس فقد فى تمويل المشروع بل أيضا بالدعم المعنوى الكبير الذى قدمته.

الشكر ممتد أيضا الى اللواتى شاركن من التوأمة البريطانية الفلسطينية خاصة توأمة هيرنجا والعيزرية، جنوب شرق لندن وبيت فوريك، تورهملت وجنين، وبالطبع كامدن وابوديس بالإضافة الى أن المشروع أدى الى انجاز توأمات جديدة مثل لاند لويس والساوية، هيستنج ويتما، ستارلنج وشعفاط ونأمل بان يكون هناك توأمة للبلدة القديمة من مدينة القدس. مع تمنياتنا بالتوفيق لكل هذة التوأمات.

الشكر الجزيل للنساء اللواتى شاركن فى المشروع، اللواتى تنقلن وساهمن بقوة فى تبادل الزيارات، ولكل من استضفن ورحبن وساعدن بشتى الطرق، وتبادلن التجارب مع المجموعة الأخرى بشكل مساعد ودافئ.

Acknowledgements

Camden Abu Dis Friendship Association and Dar Assadaqa Community Centre, Abu Dis, who organised the exchange visits, would like to thank the very many individuals, groups and women's organisations who made this possible. There were so many organisations involved in making the Stories from our Mothers project a success – please see the list on page 148-9.

We must however single out the Al Quds University Gender Studies Centre, Abu Dis, Palestine and the Centre for Gender Studies at the School of Oriental and African Studies in Camden where we held the very special Stories from our Mothers workshops during the project where many of these stories were told.

Many thanks too to the Anna Lindh Foundation for an important part of the finance for the project and beyond that for their positive support.

Thank you for your part to the following grassroots twinning groups which took a main part in the project: Haringey-Aizariya, South East London-Beit Fourik, Tower Hamlets-Jenin – and of course Camden-Abu Dis! Also thank you and good luck to those making new links that this project helped to further: Llanidloes-As Sawiya, Hastings-Yitma, Stirling-Shu'fat, and possibly – we hope – links for the Old City of Jerusalem. All of these are part of the Britain-Palestine Twinning Network.

A massive thank you to the women who took part in the project, those who travelled and contributed so strongly on the exchange visits, and to all of those who hosted and welcomed and helped in so many ways, and exchanged experiences with the other group in such a warm and hopeful way.

تقديم من كامدن
النساء من بريطانيا وفلسطين

قصص من أمهاتنا
(لقاء بين النساء من بريطانيا وفلسطين)

١

يحتوى هذا الكتاب على قصص من النساء الفلسطينيات والنساء البريطانيات، لقد بينة النساء الفلسطينيات مدى تأثر حياتهن فى كل مناحيها بةاقع الاحتلال الاسرائيلى، وقد سلطت الدكتورة فدوى اللبدى مزيد من الضوء على هذا المضوع فى تقديمها، كذلك فقد اظهرن مدى صلابتهم وإصرارهن على مواصلة حياتهن، بتقديم الدعم لاسرهن وفى متابعة دراستهن فى ظروف تكاد تكون مستحيلة.

مشاركة النساء من بريطانيا (من القوميات المختلفة) فى هذا الكتاب، جاءت كتعليقات وصور وقصص كانت بمجملها كرد فعل لما اكتشفنه عن حياة النساء الفلسطينيات تحت الاحتلال، بعض المشاركات كانت عامة وبعضها كانت ملاحظات صادمة لما شاهدن، فيما كان البعض الآخر عبارة عن قصص لحياة أمهاتهن أو جداتهن، من (بريطانيا وإسبانيا و جنوب أفريقيا) والتى مثلت مقارنه جيدة لما تمر به النساء الفلسطينيات تحت الاحتلال.

هذا الكتاب لم يكن عن مشروع قصص من أمهاتنا نفسه (هناك معلومات إضافية عن المشروع فى نهاية الكتاب). ويمكننا القول بأن المشروع حقق نجاحا مميزا.

الزيارة الاولى تزامنت مع الثانى من تشرين ثانى وهى الذكرى السنوية لوعد بلفور المشئوم عام 1917، عندما قررت الحكومة البريطانية بأن تمنح أرض فلسطين لليهود، تلك الذكرى التى حملت فى طياتها ألم ومعاناة كبيرة للفلسطينيين وأبرزت التعامل الغير منصف من قبل الحكومة البريطانية معهم.

فيما جاءت الزيارة الثانية بالتزامن مع الثامن من آذار يوم المرأة العالمى، والتى لا تعبر فقط عن التركيز على قضايا المرأة بل ولتوضح الإصرار على وجوب بناء علاقات مبنية على المساواة والاحترام بين النساء فى كل العالم.

من الممكن أن تكون هاتين المناسبتين طغتا برمزيتهما على مخرجات المشروع، لكن كان هناك العديد من النشاطات الأخرى التى استمتعت النساء من كلا البلدين فى المشاركة بها. فالطابع الاجتماعى والحياة الأسرية بالإضافة الى الأشغال اليدوية والطهى كانت أيضا حاضرة، لكن الملح كان حقيقاً للمرأة الفلسطينية هو واقع حقوق الإنسان. لقد اطلعن على الإرث التاريخى الذى طغى على العلاقة بين بريطانيا والشعب الفلسطينى وما سببه هذا الإرث من ألم ومعاناة للشعب الفلسطينى حتى يومنا هذا، وقررن بان يعملن على تغيير هذا الواقع. جاءت الحلول بضرورة الاستمرار فى بناء العلاقات بين الأفراد والمجموعات المبنية على الاحترام التبادل والمساواة واحترام مبادئ حقوق الانسان فى جميع أرجاء بريطانيا وفلسطين، وقد شعرن بأن مشروع قصص من أمهاتنا جاء ليعزز هذا التوجه ويدفعه الى الأمام.

وعليه فان متن الكتاب مثل المشروع نفسه. الصفحات الاولى جسدت بداية الحكاية. المتن كان جديا، صادم وملهم. وفى الصفحات الأخيرة لم تكن النهاية.

نديتا داوسن
منسقة
جمعية صداقة كامدن أبوديس
لندن آيار 2010.

يحتوى هذا الكتاب على مجموعة تجارب للنساء من فلسطين وبريطانيا. وقد تم جمع القصص خلال مشروع تبادل زيارات: نساء من بريطانيا زرن فلسطين فى شهر تشرين ثانى 2009 ونساء من فلسطين زرن بريطانيا فى شهر آذار 2010.

لقد تم تصميم مشروع قصص من أمهاتنا بشكل متوازن بحيث أتيح المجال للنساء من الطرفين للقاء بعضهن والتحدث عن حياتهن، وقد شاركت نساء من قطاعات مختلفة فى العمر والتجارب حيث أقمن فى بيوت بعضهن البعض فى البلدين وتنقلن فى البلدين وشاركن فى العديد من الفعاليات التى شملت جولات، وطهى طعام، وأشغال يدوية، بالإضافة الى اطلاع بعضهن البعض على الصور والأماكن المفضلة، الحديث عن هموم حياتهن والصعوبات التى يواجهنها وعن أطفالهن والدراسة والعمل.

لكن التوازن سرعان ما انتهى حيث أن الخلاف فى الحياة بين النساء من بريطانيا وفلسطين لم يكن فقط خلافا ثقافيا، النساء من فلسطين يقبعن تحت احتلال إسرائيلى (النساء البريطانيات على اختلاف عرقياتهن) لديهن مساحة اكبر من الحرية، لقد شكل ما تم اكتشافه خلال المشروع (حتى فى الجزء البريطانى منه) صدمة كبيرة للنساء البريطانيات على اعتبار أن العديد ممن شاركن فيه يعرفن عن فلسطين للمرة الاولى. لقد كان هناك رغبة شديدة عند النساء الفلسطينيات فى أن تصل تجاربهن الى خارج النطاق اللواتى يعشن فيه.

Introduction from Camden: British and Palestinian women

Stories from our Mothers

(Meetings of British and Palestinian women)

This book contains stories from experience of women from Palestine and Britain. The stories were gathered during a project of exchange visits: British women visiting Palestine in November 2009, and Palestinian women visiting Britain in March 2010.

The Stories from our Mothers project was designed with a symmetry—women met other women and talked about their lives; there were women from a range of fields, ages and experiences. In each country they visited each other's houses, travelled across the country and took part in a range of activities including tourism, cooking, craftwork, showing each other pictures and favourite places, talking about the rhythm of women's lives and their differences—childhood, studying, work, motherhood, old age.

However, there the symmetry ended. The differences between the lives of British and Palestinian lives are not just cultural. The women from Palestine are living under Israeli Occupation, and the women from Britain (with their many origins) have so much more freedom. Discovering what this meant (including the British part in it) was shocking for the British women, many of whom were learning about this for the first time. And the Palestinian women urgently wanted to make their own experiences known outside the places that they lived in.

This book includes voices from Palestinian women and from British women. The Palestinian women show how their lives are affected in every aspect by the Israeli occupation: Fadwa Al-Labadi explains more about this in her introduction. They also show their amazing determination to get on with life, support their families and succeed in study despite the hard and sometimes terrible circumstances.

The British women (from many backgrounds of course) have contributed comments, photographs and stories of their own to this book. These are responses to what they discovered about the lives of Palestinian women living under the Israeli occupation – some are journal entries, many are shocked comments, and others are stories from their own mothers' and grandmothers' lives (from Britain, Spain and South Africa) that provide a comparison to the Palestinian women's lives.

This is not a book about the Stories from our Mothers project itself (there is some information on it in the last pages of the book) but it is possible to say that it has been a great success.

The first exchange visit was at the time of the 2nd November anniversary of the 1917 Balfour Declaration, when the British government decided that the Palestinians' country could be given away. That day was a reminder of the huge pain that this has caused, and of the history of inequality between British and Palestinian people. The second exchange visit was around the 8th March International Women's Day, which represents not only a focus on women but a determination to link across the world to build equality and to work together.

Perhaps these two anniversaries symbolise the outcome of the project. The women involved enjoyed the cooking, craftwork, family sides of the visits, but the urgent concern became the issue of human rights for the Palestinian women. The women who met each other looked at the legacy of this past relation of British and Palestinian people which is the painful reality of Palestinian life now, and wanted to work for change. They resolved to build a strong, on-going relationship between individuals and groups all over Britain and Palestine which would focus on equality, respect and human rights. They felt the Stories project had helped this forward.

So the shape of this book is like the project itself. It started with a **beginning**. The **middle** was serious, shocking and motivating. And the last pages are **not the end**.

Nandita Dowson
Co-ordinator
Camden Abu Dis Friendship Association
London, May 2010

تقديم مين أبوديس: نساء تحت الاحتلال

تأثير الاحتلال الإسرائيلى واجراءاته العسكرية على قصص النساء الفلسطينيات

والضرب المباشر فى حالات اقتحام منازلهن أو أثناء حدوث مواجهات فى نفس الحى او فى حال اعتداءات المستوطنين.

العديد من النساء الحوامل وضعن مواليدهن على الحواجز أو داخل سيارات الإسعاف وفى المقاعد الخلفية لسيارات عائلاتهن بسبب احتجازهن على الحواجز وعدم السماح لهن بالعبور الى المستشفيات وقد توفى العشرات من مواليدهن لحظات بعد الولادة.

وعليه فإن المرأة الفلسطينية ستروى قصص عن السياسات الهمجية الإسرائيلية، عن القمع والاضطهاد وعن العقوبات الجماعية ضد الشعب الفلسطينى، من مصادرة أراضى وبناء مستوطنات وحواجز عسكرية والجدار الفاصل وهدم المنازل وفصل العائلات.

فى زمن الصراعات عندما يحرم الرجال من التحرك بحرية، ويجبرون على التزام منازلهم مما يسلبهم دورهم فى إعاشة وحماية عائلاتهم، تظهر بشكل جلى مساهمات المرأة والدور الهام الذى تلعبه فى الصفوف الأمامية، فتكون الأم والسجينة السياسية والمعيلة للأسرة.

من الواضح أن انخراط المرأة فى واقع النضال والصراع مكنها على ما يبدو من الخروج عن نطاق دورها المألوف.

لقد أظهرت قصص النساء الجانب الإنسانى للمأساة الفلسطينية، هؤلاء الذين فقدوا أرضهم وطردوا من بيوتهم وشردوا، ومن فقدوا أطفالهم وأفراد من أسرهم، حرى بنا أن نجمع ونوثق القصص والذكريات الفلسطينية على اعتبار أن هذه القصص جاءت من قطاعات وأجيال مختلفة. وتحديداً من عاشوا فصول النكبة الذين لازالوا على قيد الحياة من الأجداد والآباء الذين ينقلون تجاربهم وقصصهم للأجيال الجديدة

باعتقادى أن ما روى من قصص للنساء برغم من أنها قصص فردية إلا أنها تروى قصص المجتمع، على اعتبار أن تجارب النساء من الممكن أن تكون المرآة التى تعكس تجارب شعب كامل.

لقد جسدت تجارب النساء الأكبر سناً عقود من الحياة تحت الاحتلال الإسرائيلى، او كلاجئات فى المنافى يستذكرن بيوتهن وتجربة التشرد عن الوطن. يتذكرن الفترة ما قبل النكبة كما ويتذكرن جيدا النكبة نفسها، فهن من خلال سردهن لتجاربهن يسلطن الضوء على قصة شعب بكامله، كل قصة شخصية تعكس الذاكرة الجماعية للمعاناة جيل كامل وتشكل رافعة فى تحفيز الأجيال على الاستمرار فى النضال من أجل البقاء.

إن فقدان المنازل، والوطن والتشرد الذى عاشوه عكس فى طياته ذكريات حلوة ومرة فى أذهان الأجيال المتعاقبة.

دكتور فدوى اللبدى
مدير مركز إنسان لدراسات الجندر
جامعة القدس

مكن التاريخ المحكى (المروى) من تسليط الضوء بشكل دقيق على تجارب النساء والطبيعة الخاصة لهذه التجارب، وعلى الرغم من أنه لم يتم حفظ وتوثيق ونشر هذه القصص إلا أن النمط الروائى فى سرد القصص من النساء فى بريطانيا وفلسطين يساهم فى انتقال هذه القصص من جيل الى جيل.

لقد كان التركيز على العناصر المهمشة فى ذاكرة النساء، وبالتحديد للنساء الفلسطينيات اللواتى ومنذ مطلع القرن العشرين حتى وقتنا الحالى يعملن جاهدات فى كل ميادين الحياة من أجل حقوقهن كنساء من جهة ومن أجل قضيتهن الوطنية من جهة أخرى. لقد كن ضحايا للسياسات الوحشية الإسرائيلية. وبشكل بارز فى التعامل مع فقدان الأقارب الذين قتلوا أو اعتقلوا خلال الحرب، ورعاية الجرحى من أفراد العائلة ممن أدت إصاباتهم الى إعاقات استوجبت عناية خاصة.

وكباقى أبناء الشعب الفلسطينى فقد تعرضت المرأة الفلسطينية للقتل والإصابة على أيدى قوات الاحتلال، استشهدت العديد من النساء جراء إصابتهن بالرصاص الحى والقصف المفاجئ وإطلاق الصواريخ على بيوتهن والأحياء السكنية التى يعشن بها. كذلك فقد تعرضن للإصابات والاعتقال جراء مشاركتهن فى المقاومة والعمليات الاستشهادية دفاعا عن الوطن، يضاف الى ذلك معاناة النساء الحوامل اللواتى يتعرضن الى الرش بالغاز المسيل للدموع

4

Introduction from Abu Dis: Women under Occupation

The impact of the Israeli occupation and its military actions on Palestinian women's stories

Oral histories have been especially useful in highlighting the particular experiences of women and the gendered nature of their experience. Drawing on oral history narratives of Palestinian and British women's stories, these stories passed from one generation to another are undocumented narratives that have not been sufficiently explored in literature. The focus is on the somewhat neglected dimension of women's memories, particularly those of Palestinian women who since the early 20th century and through to the present day have been striving in different spheres of life both for their rights as women and for their people's national independence. They have shared the burden of Israel's brutal policies, most saliently in coping with the loss of relatives killed or imprisoned during the war, and in looking after injured family members who became disabled and require special care.

Like other Palestinians, women too, are killed and injured by Israeli occupation forces. Many women are killed from the use of live ammunition and the sudden shelling and missile attacks over their neighborhood. They are also injured, imprisoned, and become human-bombs. Moreover, pregnant women are exposed to gas inhalation or are directly hit due to the proximity of their houses to flashpoints where clashes take place, or to Jewish settlements. Dozens of women have given birth at checkpoints and of these deliveries inside ambulances and in the backs of their cars, tens of stillborn babies have died during or soon after birth.

Therefore Palestinian women's stories tell about the Israelis' severe policies, oppression, repression and collective punishments against the Palestinians such as confiscation of land, settlement construction, checkpoints, construction of the Separation Wall demolition of houses and dispossession of families. During a time of conflict where men are deprived of access to mobility, forced to stay at home and not any more to meet their traditionally ascribed roles as breadwinners and protectors of the family, women make a clear contribution as front liners: mothers, political prisoners, breadwinners. The challenging and conflicting reality on the ground seems to give space and opportunity for women to act as agents and go beyond the boundaries of the domestic space.

The women's stories articulate the human aspects of the Palestinian disaster, those people who lost their land, expelled from their houses and became displaced, who lost their children and other members of their families and neighbours. It is significant to document the Palestinian stories and memories because these stories bear out from several social groups and different successive generations, those who lived at the Nakba time and are still alive, grandparents and parents pass the history on for the new generation.

I believe that women's self-narration is based on collective, not individual, identity. The personal experiences of women mirror the reality of a whole people. Older women recalling the many decades during which they have lived under Israeli occupation or as refugees in exile remember their homes and the experience of dispossession. They memorize the periods immediately before the Nakba as well as the Nakba itself. They tend to tell their stories in terms of telling the nation's story: each individual's story reflects the collective memory of the suffering of Palestinian generations and telling them inspires and helps the new generation to struggle and survive. Thus the loss of their houses, homeland and the coerced displacement have carried and reflected sweet and bitter memories down to the successive generations.

Fadwa Al-Labadi,
Director of Insan Centre for Gender Studies,
Al-Quds University

5

الـبـــدايـــة

The beginning

الانطباع الاول

لقد كان من الصعب أن اصدق ما رأيت وسمعت، لقد زرت إسرائيل مرتين فى الماضى ولم يتسنى لى معرفة ما يجرى، لقد تمكنت فى هذه الزيارة من استكشاف الحقائق بطريقة عرضية لم أكن اخطط لها.انه فعلا مخطط مدروس لطرد الفلسطينيين من مدينة القدس وأجزاء أخرى فى الضفة الغربية.... ولن أبالغ اذا قلت انه نظام فصل عنصرى. هناك جدار بارتفاع ثمانى أمتار مع حواجز عسكرية مثبته عليه يطوق القرى والبلدات وفى العديد من الحالات يفصل العائلات الذين اجبروا على حمل بطاقات هوية مختلفة الألوان تخولهم العيش فى مناطق محددة. يمكنك أن ترى بوضوح بان المناطق الفلسطينية تحولت الى جيتوهات (معازل) شبيهه بما عاناه اليهود فى ألمانيا النازية، من الصعب أن تصدق بان التاريخ يعيد نفسه وان الضحية قد أصبحت الجلاد.

لقد التقينا خلال الرحلة بالعديد من الناس الذين اخبرونا عن قصصهم وقد كان ملفتاً جداً أن ترى روح الصمد والتحديد والصدق الذى تجلى عند الكثيرون منهم. لقد كانوا صريحين وصادقين عن الانقسام الحاصل فى مجتمعهم وفى تعبيرهم عن خيبة أملهم بقياداتهم. إحدى النساء تحدثت فى الأمس قائله: (يستطيعون اخذ معطفى وشجرات الزيتون وارضى ولكن لن يستطيعوا تدمير

معنوياتى) وهذا دليل واضح على الصمود، إحدى النساء الكبيرات فى السن والتى عاشت الكثير من المعاناة كانت ملهمة جداً للمجموع، لقد بدت النساء الفلسطينيات مثقفات تواقات الى نقل قصص معاناتهن إلينا جميعاً والى العالم لنشاهد ونسمع عما يحدث فى فلسطين.

هناك الكثير لأروى واكتب، أنا أناضل لاستوعب وافهم ما شاهدت وسمعت، يبدو أن هناك كثير من الفظائع القادمة من إسرائيل فى سبيل تحويل القدس لمدينة يهودية. لقد كانت المجموعة التى رافقتها الى فلسطين مميزة جداً وقد شاركت فى العديد من النقاشات التى غيرت الكثير فى نفسى لا توجد لدى الآن أى فكرة عن التحركات التى انوى القيام بها من اجل التغيير ولكنى الآن بدأت استوعب ما يحدث.

الطقس بارد ومبتل هنا...... ولم أجد الدفىء الذى تهيئة له...

جين ريديفورد [بريطانيا]

8

النساء اللواتى زرن أبوديس من بريطانيا تمكن من الذهاب الى القدس (هذة الصورة التقطت بجانب باب العامود) لكن صديقاتهن من فلسطين لم يتمكن من الدخول الى القدس ومرافقتهن عبر الحاجز الإسرائيلى.

Women visitors to Abu Dis were able to go to Jerusalem but their Palestinian friends were not allowed to go through the Israeli checkpoint with them

First impressions

It is hard to believe that I have been to Israel twice and had no idea what was going on and that I only stumbled across it more by accident then my own intention. It is a very conscious system of squeezing out the Palestinians from Jerusalem and many parts of the West Bank... and not too extreme to say a form of apartheid. There is a series of huge 8 metre concrete walls with checkpoints that have been built encircling villages, and in many cases dividing families, who have to have special pass cards of different colours to go into different places. As you can imagine they are turning into a form of ghetto... similar to what the Jews must have experienced in Germany, hard to believe how history repeats itself, and the victim turns into the oppressor.

We have met with many people who have told us their stories, and it is humbling to see the spirit and steadfastness that is shining through many of the people, also the honesty. They are straightforward and honest about the division amongst their own people, and the distrust of their own leadership. One woman spoke with passion yesterday... saying "They can take away my coat, my olives, my land, but not my mind or my spirit" – and this is evident. Some of the older woman, who have obviously seen so much, are very inspiring, they seem highly educated and fired with an intense passion to get the word out to all of us and the world community – as eyes and ears to what is going on.

There is too much to write, and I am also struggling to digest and process it all... It seems that so much horror is coming from Israel's determination to make Jerusalem a wholly Jewish place. The group I have come with are great – and I have had a few conversations that touched on a deeper territory and spirit of change, I have no idea how I will respond to all this... but for now I am just absorbing.

Cold and wet here... not the heat I was imagining and came prepared for....

Jane Riddiford [UK]

الـــلاجـئيـــن

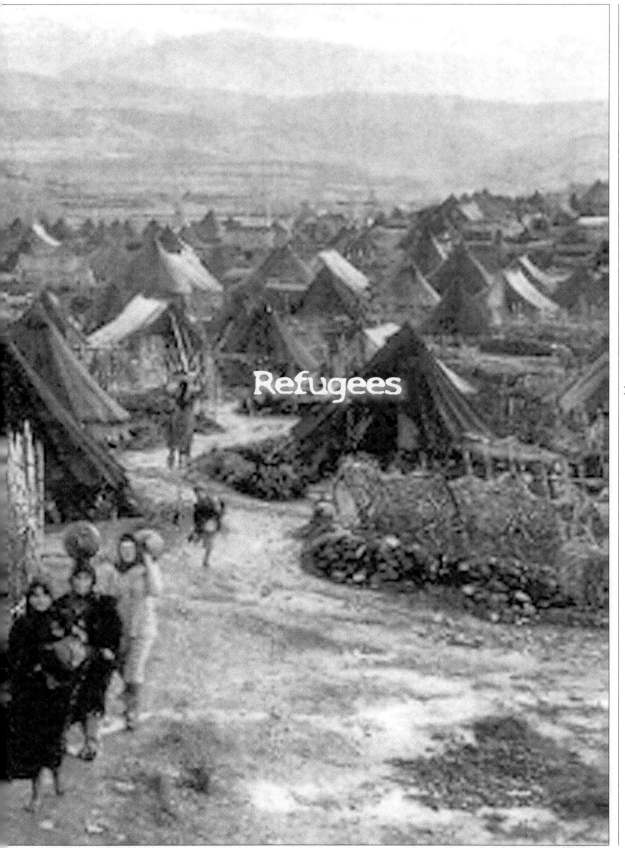

Refugees

خلف الجبال

قصةٌ من اسبانيا خلال حكم فرانكو

أحب أمي كثيراً، الجميع أحب أمي، لديها جاذبيةٌ عالية، كأنها منع للحب.

أظن أن مرد ذلك الطفولة القاسية التي عاشتها، تعلمت أن تقدر هذا الشيء وأن ما يسعدنا من الممكن أن يكون بسيطاً جداً، الحب يجعلنا سعداء وكلما أعطينا فى الحب أكثر كلما حصلنا عليه أكثر.

ولدت أمي فى مدينة برشلونة فى العام 1937 ، خلال الحرب الأهلية، جدى كان جندى فى الجيش الجمهورى الذى حارب فى ذلك الوقت فى مقاطعة كتلونيا، فى جنوب إسبانيا على الحدود مع فرنسا، يحارب من أجل الديمقراطية ضد النظام الفاشى.

بعد أن هزموا فى الحرب، فر مئات الآلاف من الجمهوريين الى فرنسا، لقد أجبر هؤلاء الناس على ترك بلدهم التى حاربوا لأجلها ببسالة، وهزموا أمام الدكتاتور فرانكو.

كان عمر أمى الثالثة عشر شهراً وكانت جدتى حامل فى شهرها الخامس، وقد قطع أبى جبال البرنيس مشيا على الأقدام مع الآلاف الناس.

لم ترحب فرنسا بالذين حاربوا وانضموا للمقاومة ممن نزحوا الى أرضها، وضع الرجال فى معسكرات احتجاز، والنساء والأطفال وضعوا فى إصلاحيات وسجون.

أنجبت جدتى طفلةً أخرى فى فرنسا ولم تصلها أى أخبار من جدى على مدار سنتين، بعد ذلك تمكنت من العودة مرة أخرى الى إسبانيا.

عاشت أمى مع جديها فى بلدة صغيرة خارج مدينة مدريد لمدة سبع سنوات، وعلى الرغم من المآسى التى خلفتها الحرب تذكر أمى بأن هذة السنوات كانت الأجمل فى حياتها. دلل الجدين أحفادهم وتمتعت الطفلتان فى جو الريف المسالم.

بعد سبع سنوات تمكن جدى من الهرب من معسكر الاحتجاز، وعاد الى أسرته التى قررت مغادرة الريف والتوجه للعيش فى مدينة مدريد ليختفي جدى فى زحمة المدينة ولا يتعرف عليه أحد حتى لا تتم معاقبته واعتقاله مرةً أخرى.

لم يتعافى جدى أبداً من عقدة الحرب. لقد كانت فترة صعبة جداً، حيث أصبح جدى صامتاً فى معظم الوقت لم يشأ أن ينقل ما فى قلبه من حقد وكره لقلوب أولاده.

جدتى خلقت جدار حول نفسها وقررت عدم الاكتراث بأحد ألا نفسها، أخرجت أمى وخالتى من المدرسة ودفعت بهما الى العمل وهن فى سن الثانية عشر والثالثة عشر.

أصبحت أمى الروح والقلب لعائلتها، الروح القوية والقلب الدافئ، والذى افتقده أهلها خلال الحرب.

استمرت أمى حتى الآن بتوزيع الاهتمام والمحبة يومياً على العديد من الناس، هى من ذاك النوع من الناس الذى يجعلك تشعر بالارتياح لمجرد تواجدها معك. آمل أن يمتد عمرها أكثر وأكثر، لأن الشيء الوحيد الذى لم تعلمني إياه هو كيف يمكن أن أحيا بدون وجودها.

ميلا كامبوى [بريطانيا]

Over the mountains

A story from Spain under Franco

I love my mum a lot. Everybody loves my mother. She has such a calming effect, it's like she irradiates love.

I think because her childhood was hard, she learned to appreciate that the things that make us happy are simple. Love made us happy and the more that we give, the more that we have.

My mother was born in Barcelona in 1937, in the middle of a civil war. Her father, a republican soldier, was fighting at the time in Catalonia, in the northeast of Spain on the border with France, defending the democracy from the fascist occupation.

After they were defeated, hundreds of thousands of Republicans fled to France. Those people were forced to leave the country they had fought for so fiercely, defeated by dictator Franco.

My mother was thirteen months old and my grandmother was five months pregnant. My family along side thousands of other people crossed the Pyrenees by foot.

There was no welcome in France for the heroes of the resistance. The men were put in concentration camps and the women and children in improvised prison.

My grandmother had another daughter there and she waited, without news from my grandfather, for two long years. After that she managed to come back to Spain. My mother lived with her grandparents in a small town just outside Madrid for the next seven years. Despite the miseries of the post-war, my mother remembers those years as happy times. Her grandparents spoilt their grand-daughters and the girls enjoyed the peaceful country life.

After seven years my grandfather managed to escape from the concentration camp, he was reunited with his family and they decided to go and live in Madrid where nobody knew them to avoid any more punishment.

My grandfather never recovered from the war. It was hard for him to face the daily humiliation of accepting the occupation. He became a quiet guy that muttered often against the fascists but not too loud because he didn't want to sow hatred in his children's hearts.

My grandmother created a wall around her and decided not to worry about anybody else but herself. She took my aunt and my mother out of school and put then to work when they were twelve and thirteen. My mother become the soul and heart for the family, the strong soul and the warm heart that her parents lost during the war.

My mother continues even now to spread care and love daily to lots of people, she is the kind of person that makes you feel better just by being there. I hope she is going to be there for a long, long time, because one thing that she never taught me is how to survive without her.

Mila Campoy [UK]

13

قصة أمي

أنا أصلاً من قرية فى شمال فلسطين اسمها عيلبون حيث وقعت مذبحة فى قريتنا فى العام ١٩٤٨ قصة أمى أنها كانت حامل بشهرها التاسع وعندها طفل عمره سنة.

حين دخل الصهاينة الى بلدتنا عيلبون اخرج الرجال من البيوت وكان من ضمن من اخرجوا زوجها وشقيقها وشقيق زوجها بالإضافة الى ستة عشر رجل من البلدة، وتضيف أمى أنها سمعت إطلاق النار بعد فترة من اقتياد الرجال كانت مجزرة حقيقية حيث قتل الرجال جميعا باستثناء أبى الذى أرغم على السير أمام جنود العصابات الصهيونية لخوفهم من وجود الألغام او أطلاق النار وقد استطاع فيما بعد يلحق بأمى الى لبنان.

توصف أمى المشهد عند الخروج حيث سمعت صوت إطلاق النار على أخيها، سيدة أخرى قتلوا زوجها ولم تستطيع أن تودعه طلبت من الله أن يرحمه وتابعت المسير وثالثه لم تستطع حمل ابنتها فتركتها ولم تعرف ما حل بها، ورابعة لم تستطع حمل ابنتها من التعِب فتركتها فحملها رجل كان بالقرب منها، كان المشهد رهيباً ولم يستطع احد منهم فعل شىء.

وصلوا الى لبنان بعد معاناة مشى على الأقدام فى البرد أنجبت أمى طفلة هناك بلبنان القارص وكان التاريخ 30/10 وهى لا زالت تبكى على حالتها وحالة أهلها ... بعد مرور أشهر أهلى الى عيلبون، ادعى الكثيرون بان أهالى بلدة عيلبون محظوظون بالعودة لأنها قرية بأغلبية مسيحية وان الصهاينة تعاملوا مع المسيحيين بشكل مختلف، لكن الواقع

مختلف فهم دمروا عيلبون لقد استهدفوا كل الفلسطينيين بدون النظر الى طوائفهم ومعتقداتهم.

كانت الهجمة شرسة جداً صحيح أن هناك من استطاع العودة لكن لازال العديدين بالانتظار لا يكاد يخلى بيت او عائلة من أقارب لهم يعيشون فى لبنان يحلمون بالعودة الى عيلبون.

أنا سعيدة جداً لوجود وعى نسوى الآن لأننى أتذكر فى العام 1980 عندما بدأنا مع مجموعة من شبان بلدة عيلبون بجمع القصص حول ما حدث فى عام 1948 وقد تحدثت الى من عاش تلك الفترة ابتداءً من أبى الذى افتقد لقصصه الآن لأنه رحل منذ فترة، لم يكن لدى الوعى الكافى وكل ما كنا نجمع كان يتعلق بما واجهه الرجال من قتل وإبادة ولم نكن لنلتفت لما عانته المرأة من ألم وعذاب فى تلك المرحلة.

نقطة أخرى مهمة الآن يوجد العديدة من المتاحف فى إسرائيل توثق لما حدث فى العام 1948 ولكن لا ذكر فى هذة المتاحف لأى معلومات عن ما حدث للفلسطينيون وما عانوه من قتل وتهجير وعن ما عاناه أبى وعائلتى وأهلى فى عيلبون.

وفى كل مرة نزور بها متاحف بإسرائيل نطالبهم بان يكون هناك معلومات عن ما حدث تأتى الإجابة بأنه لا يوجد تمويل لجمع وأرشفة هذة القصص.

وفاء شريق

من كلمة ألقتها خلال ورشة عمل مشروع قصص من أمهاتنا فى جامعة القدس تشرين ثانى 2009

14

My mother's story

I am originally from a village in the north called Ailaboun. A massacre took place in our village in 1948 and its people fled to Lebanon.

My mother's story is that she was pregnant then, in the ninth month of her pregnancy. She also had a son who was one year old. When the Zionists entered our village, Ailaboon, they forced the men to go out of their houses. They took her husband and his brother and her own brother together with sixteen other men from the village. My mother said that some time after the soldiers took the men, she heard gun shots. It was very horrible because all the men were killed, except my father. He was forced to walk in front of the soldiers to protect them in case there were any bombs or gunshots against them. My father managed to survive and follow my mother after that to Lebanon.

My mother described the scene when she went out. She heard the guns shooting her brother but no one was able to do anything. The husband of another woman was shot and she did not manage to say goodbye to him, she just asked God to have mercy on him and kept on walking. Another woman was not able to carry her daughter so she left her behind and no one knew where she was or what happened to her. A fourth woman was not able to carry her daughter because she was too tired so she left her but a man came and carried her. It was very terrible, nobody managed to do anything to stop what was happening.

They walked together till they got to Lebanon. It was very hard, they suffered pain and cold. They arrived on 30th October and my mother gave birth there, in Lebanon, to a girl. She was still crying because of the situation that she and her family found themselves in.

Some months later, my family managed to return to Ailaboun. People used to say that the people of Ailaboun were lucky because they returned back. But the reason was that the village had a Chrisian majority and that the Zionists used to deal with Christians in a better way than they treated Muslims. But I want to say that they destroyed the whole village and that Zionists target all Palestinians without looking at their religions or their sects.

The attack was very hard. It is right that many people managed to return, but still more waited. It is very hard to find one house or one family in Ailaboon without relatives who are in Lebanon, dreaming of returning to Ailaboun.

I am very happy to find that there is now a general an awareness of women: I remember in 1980, when I started to collect stories about what happened in 1948 together with people in Ailaboun, I spoke to people who lived in that period, starting with my own father – I miss his stories now as he passed away some time ago – I remember that I did not have enough awareness, and we all collected stories from what the men faced in that period: killing and death, and we did not take account of the suffering of the women in that period.

Another point about stories from that time is that in Israel there are museums in Israel about the history of 1948, but they do not ever mention what happened to the Palestinians, to my father or my family or the people of Ailaboun who were killed or forced to leave their land.

When I ask people in these museums why they don't have such stories, or indeed a whole archive about them, they usually say that is a question of money.

Wafa Shreiq

From a talk at the Stories from our Mothers workshop at Al Quds University, Abu Dis, November 2009

مسيرة أيام

حدثتني إحدى الأمهات فقالت:

كنا نعيش في بيت جميل وبساتين مزروعة حول البيت ملكاً لأسرتي، أنا كنت أكبر إخوتي كان عمري 12 عاماً وقد كنا سعداء بهذا البيت الذي يضم أسرتي.

ساد الذعر في البلدة وخرجنا في الليل كل واحد منا يحمل بطانية يتغطى بها تركنا كل شيء على أمل الرجوع عن قريب. ساد الذعر في البلدة وخرجنا في الليل كل واحد منا يحمل بطانية يتغطى به تركنا كل شيء على أمل الرجوع عن قريب.

لم استطع حمل لحافي الثقيل فحملته أمي، وصلنا الى كروم العنب والتين القريبة من قريتنا الجورة.

مكثنا في البساتين حوالي عشرة أيام، باستثناء رجل يدعى قدوم رفض أن يخرج من بيته في البلدة وقد سمعنا انه قتل بصاروخ أطلقه الصهاينة من الشرفة (شرفة عين كارم)واستشهد في بيته.

تسلل بعض الأهالي ودفنوه على عجل ودون أن يجروا أي مراسم للدفن.

بعد تلك الحادثة رحلنا الى قرية رأس أبو عمار نمشي بين الجبال ونحن نحمل الملابس وأواني الطبخ والبطانيات مكثنا في رأس أبو عمار من 20-25 يوم، وبعدها وصلت أخبار بان عصابات الصهاينة في طريقها الى القرية، غادرنا القرية في الليل مشياً على الأقدام لمسافة طويلة جداً قاصدين مدينة بيت لحم.

لم تكن الرحلة سهلة فقد استمرت ثلاث أيام لم نتمكن من الحصول على الطعام او الراحة ولم يكن لدينا طحين لنعجنه.

وصلنا بيت لحم وخرج أبي ليجد لنا مكاناً او (خشة) تأوينا وتركنا تحت الأشجار في بلدة الخضر، بدأت السماء تمطر علينا ونحن في العراء، وجد والدي خشة صغيرة لا تصلح للسكن سكناها وكان المطر يتسرب إليها، كان البرد شديد وليس معنا ملابس دافئة ولا شيء.

قدم إلينا رهبان من (السريان) احضروا لنا الطعام وأعطونا بعض الأغطية والملابس، بعد ذلك قرر والدي التوجه الى القدس والبحث عن منزل لنا هناك.

بعد فترة أيام تركنا بيت لحم وتوجهنا الى صور باهر وبعد ذلك الى باب الاسباط حيث جلسنا لنستريح من القصف الصهيوني بدأ على مدينة القدس سقطت مجموعة قنابل على منازل السكان واستشهدت ثلاث عائلات بكامل أفرادها وبدأ أهالي مدينة القدس بالهرب ولكن والدي قرر أن نبقى فيها وقد سكنا في غرفة صغيرة جداً في باب السلسلة.

في تلك الأيام بدت مدينة القدس خالية هجرها سكانها خوفاً من مذابح الصهاينة، بقينا في القدس وبدأ الناس يعودون إليها.

لا استوعب حتى اللحظة كيف كان نزوحنا مشياً على الأقدام من قرية الى قرية.... بقينا في القدس أربعون عاماً حتى استطعنا شراء قطعة ارض صغيرة في ابوديس، حتى الآن احلم ببيتي الجميل الدافئ والمزرعة والبستان في قريتي الجورة أراها كثيراً في أحلامي ولكن هل ستتحقق أحلامي في العودة قبل أن أموت ..... أصبح عمري الآن ثلاثة وسبعون عاماً ولا يزال مفتاح البيت معي أحتفظ به

سحر عريقات

16

Days of walking

One of the mothers told me this story:

We were living in a very beautiful house with fields around us. It was owned by my family. I was the oldest of my brothers and sisters. I was twelve years old. All the family were happy in our house.

One day, a man came from the mountain next to our village, which is called Al Joura, close to Ein Karim. When the man arrived in our village, he started to shout "Go out of your village! Take out the women and the children! The Zionist troops are on the way to the village to kill everybody in it!"

The people were terrified, and all of them left the village in the night. They took what they could carry. Everybody took a blanket and they left the rest in the houses, hoping they would soon return.

For myself, I didn't manage to carry my blanket – it was heavy, so my mother carried it for me.

We got to the orchard and we stayed there ten days. One man from the village – his name was Qdoum – refused to leave his house in the village, and we heard after that that a Zionist rocket came, thrown from Al Sharafet Ein Karim, and the man was killed inside his house.

Some of the people from the village went back under cover of darkness and buried him; then they came back to the orchard.

After that, we all moved to another village called Ras Abu Ammar, and we spent between twenty and twenty-five days there, till the news arrived at that village too that the Zionist gangs were on their way to the village. Everybody left the village, walking on their feet, for a very long distance, going to Bethlehem town.

It was not an easy trip to Bethlehem: we spent three nights walking, and we did not have food or anything with us; we didn't even have flour to make bread.

We arrived at a village called Al Khader, near Bethlehem, where my father left us under the trees, and went to Bethlehem town to try to find a place for us to stay. It started raining. We were under trees and it was not easy to keep dry.

My father managed to come back that day and take us to a small hut. We went there, and even inside it we were not protected from rain. There were no warm clothes to wear and nothing to eat. Some Syrian Christian priests came to us, and gave us food and blankets and clothes.

After a few days, my father decided we should go to Jerusalem, even if it was the east side *[they came from the west of the city]*. After a few days we left Bethlehem and we went to Sour Bahar and after that to Bab al-Isbat, where we sat down to have a rest and then the Zionist bombs started to reach that side of the city.

One bomb fell on a house and three families were killed. And so the people from the east of Jerusalem also started to run away. But my father decided that we should not leave and we must stay in the city. He managed to find us a small room in a small area called Bab al-Silsila.

The city of Jerusalem was nearly empty. The people in the city were terrified by the Zionist massacres that took place in different places in the west. They left, but after a short time, people started to return.

I still till now can't imagine how we managed to walk all this distance on our feet from one village to another. We stayed in Jerusalem for forty years till we managed to buy a small piece of land in Abu Dis, and we built a house and moved there.

Until today, I still dream of our beautiful warm house and our farm in Al Joura village. The question really is whether my dreams of returning will come to reality before the end of my life. I am now seventy-three years old and I still keep the key of my house with me.

Sahar Eriqat

من حارة الشرف

الأقدام، اذكر أننى كنت احمل العجين وامشى الى الفرن فى القدس، وكنا نشترى احتياجاتنا من القدس من باب الخليل، لم يكن فى المخيم شبكة مياه عدا مجمع ماء كبير مثل العين نحمل حصتنا من الماء على رؤوسنا او بأيدينا، والمراحيض كانت مجمعات مشتركة للرجال والنساء والشخص الذى لا يستطيع أن يصبر يذهب بعيدا الى العراء ليقضى حاجته، لم يكن كذلك هناك شبكة صرف صحى.

عدد العائلات بالمخيم ممن اجبروا على مغادرة حارة الشرف كان 500 عائلة أما الآن فيوجد فى المخيم 50 ألف نسمة يعيشون فى مساحة دونمان ونصف.

لم يكن هناك كهرباء فى المخيم ولم تكن المدارس أيضا مناسبة فقد كانت باردة جدا فى الشتاء مع وجود تسريب لمياه المطر من كل مكان وبالصيف حر شديد وكانت المدرسة للصف الاول الإعدادى بعد ذلك على الطالب أن ينتقل الى مدارس القدس.

بعد سنة على ترحيلنا من حارة الشرف حصلت الحرب عام 1967 حيث سقط ما تبقى من فلسطين فى أيدى إسرائيل، بعد أسبوعين من انتهاء الحرب ذهبت لأرى بيتنا فوجدته مسكون من قبل عائلة يهودية إسرائيلية.

ليلى الشريف

أنا من مخيم شعفاط ولدت فى حارة الشرف داخل أسوار القدس ، أبى كان لاجئ من قرى جنوب الخليل أتى الى القدس وعمل فى الحرس الوطنى إبان الإنتداب البريطانى فى سنة 1943.

أصيب والدى فى رأسه أثناء حرب عام 1948 تم وضعه فى المستشفى على اعتبار انه ميت وعندما جاء الناس فى الصباح ليدفنوه اكتشفوا انه لازال حيا، نقلوه الى المستشفى الهسبيس بجانب الحرم القدسى الشريف حيث أجريت له عملية جراحية.

تبين بعد العملية أن أبى لديه حالة صرع وتم تحويله الى مستشفى القصر العينى بمصر حيث بقى تحت العلاج من عام 1951–1954 وبعدها تزوج وأنا ثانى بنت فى العائلة ولدت فى أواخر عام 1954.

الهجرة : اخبرنى والدى أن عائلتنا هاجرت من النبى داوود الى حارة الشرف وكانت هذة أول هجرة، أول هجرة من جنوب الخليل الى القدس (هجرة النبى داوود (بعدها من باب الخليل الى حارة الشرف التى تسمى اليوم حارة اليهود نحن نسميها حارة الشرف عشنا فيها من سنة 1951-1954.

بعدها تم بناء مخيم شعفاط فى منطقة مملوكه لأهالى بلدة شعفاط استأجرها الملك حسين لمدة 99 سنة وتم ترحيلنا وأجبرنا على العيش على هذا المخيم.

كانت حصة عائلتى بيت بمساحة 7 متر بطول 14 متر على اعتبار أن عدد أفراد العائلة كبير وأما العائلات الأصغر كانت المساحة المخصصة لهم 3.5 بطول 14 متر.

عندما خرجنا من حارة الشرف كان عمرى 12 سنة، أغلقنا باب بيتنا بالمفتاح وأخذنا المفتاح معنا وتركنا بعض الأغراض بالبيت وبعد أسبوعين عدنا الى البيت فوجدنا بيتنا مغلق وأغراضنا بالخارج.

لم تكن الحياة فى المخيم سهلة كنا نعد العجين بالبيت ونحمله الى فرن بالقدس لخبزه مشيا على

From Harat al-Sharaf

I now live in Shu'fat Camp. I was born in a place called Harat al-Sharaf inside the walls of Jerusalem. My father was in the National Guard in Gaza under the British Mandate in 1943. My father was a refugee from the south of Hebron and he came to Jerusalem and entered into the National Guard.

He got a bullet in his head in 1948 and he was put in the hospital as if dead. In the morning, when they came to bury him, they discovered that he was still breathing. They took him to the Hospice which is a hospital in Jerusalem, near the Al Aqsa mosque. They operated on him and he had a sort of epileptic fit. They transferred him into a hospital called Al Qasr al-Ein, in Egypt. He was there in the hospital from 1948 to 1951.

After that, he got married; I was the second daughter of his marriage. I was born at the end of 1954.

My father told me that our first emigration was from Al Nabi Dahoud, near Hebron, to Bab al-Khaleel in Jerusalem, and then we moved to Harat al-Sharaf. It is now called the Jewish Quarter but we still call it Harat al-Sharaf. We were there between 1951 and 1966. After that, Shu'fat Refugee Camp was built for the refugees on the land of people of Shu'fat village: King Hussein rented it for 99 years.

They put us in a small area: 7 metres by 14 metres. This was for a big family; smaller families had a space 3.5 metres by 14 metres. We went to the camp; Harat al-Sharaf and our houses there were taken by Jewish Israeli families.

I remember that when we left I was 12 years old. We closed the door with a key and we took the key with us. We left some of our things in the house and after two weeks we returned to the house. We found our house locked and our things thrown outside; Jews were living there.

Life was not easy in the camp. It wasn't possible to cook bread there. I used to prepare the dough in the house in the camp and go on foot, carrying it, to the bread oven in Jerusalem. We used to buy our things from Bab al-Khaleel in Jerusalem.

There was no sewage system in the camp and no water, except a large water reservoir, like a spring. We used to carry the water on our heads or in our hands. The toilets were also a problem. There were shared toilets for men and women. Anyone who couldn't wait to go to the toilet had to go outside. Five hundred came to the camp from Harat al-Sharaf; now 50,000 people live there on only 2.5 dunams of land.

There was also no electricity; we used to use oil lamps. It was difficult for schools too – they had water leaking from the ceiling. In the summer it was very hot. There was only primary school. When students reached the age of twelve, they had to go to Jersualem if they wanted to continue in education.

One year after we were moved to Shu'fat Refugee Camp, the 1967 war broke out. The Israelis took hold of the Harat al-Sharaf quarter permanently. With this large number of people in the refugee camp, the health clinics became a disaster.

Layla Al Sharif

19

قنديل الزيت

ما زالت صورةُ «عوف» تستوقفني بثوبها الفلسطيني الأسود المطرز بالأحمر والأخضر، ونطاقها الأحمر القاني المشدود إلى خصرها النحيل، ذلك الثوب الذى يضم القامةُ الممشوقةُ بعمر الشباب اليافع، ولا زلت أذكر غطاء رأسها الأبيض الذى يُلَفُّ حول وجنتين حمراوين وجبين لوّحته الشمس بلون السمرة... وعيون سوداء فيها حدةٌ وجرأةٌ، وشعر أسود منساب يُرى القليل منه عندما تشد خرقتها البيضاء لتلفها حول فمها وذقنها استحياءً من الحصادين الذين راحت مناجلهم تقطع سنابل القمح بلا هوادة.

لم تكن «عوف» الوحيدةُ اللاقطةُ لسنابل القمح في مرج ابن عامر بل شاركها الكثير من الصبايا في مثل سنها أو أكبر. مرج ابن عامر ذلك السهل الممتد عبر الأفق بين جبين الناصرة وحيفا جنةٌ من الأرض وصدر رؤوم لمن سعى في البحث عن لقمة العيش ممن شردوا ظلما وجورا من وطنهم.

أحببت «عوف» وأحببت مرج ابن عامر.... وسنابل القمح الذهبية المتراقصة والمتناغمة عندما يداعبها نسيم البحر في المساء، وأحببت أغاني الحصادين، لذا كنت شديدة الالتصاق بعوف أجمع معها بعض السنابل المتساقطةُ خلفها أو تلك التى تبعثرت من أيدى الحصادين لنضعها سوياً في كيس كبير تحمله «عوف» بعد عناء يوم صيفى إلى بيتها فتفرغه لتعود لملئه في اليوم التالى.

لم تكن أحلام «عوف» كأحلام الصبايا أن تتزوج وتنجب البنين والبنات فلم تكن لتحدث رجلاً ممن يعملون معها إلا قليلا ولم تكن لتغنى أهازيج الحصاد كبقية الصبايا من أترابها

أحدق في عينها.. فأجد الكبرياء المجروح، أنظر إلى وجهها فلم أتحسس سوى الحزن وجهها كبرًكان يمكن أن يثور في

أى لحظة.. لا تتحدث إلا قليلا فصمتها بليغ، تجلس وقت تناول الطعام إلى جذع شجرة، شاردةُ الذهن تعبث بسوار فضى كان على معصمها وعندما تمل العبث تتساقط على وجنتيها الموردتين دموع غزيرة... تحاول إخفاءها بسرعة بطرف «خرقتها» قبل أن يراها أحد...، ولكنى أسرّب نظراتى وأراقبها وأبحث عن سر هذه الدموع التى تتساقط كحبات اللؤلؤ مع حبات العرق المتدحرجةُ من جبينها لتنساب معاً بالتحام وانسجام.

انقضى موسم الحصاد وحمّلت الغلةُ من البيدر على عربات خشبيةٌ تجرها الخيول والحمير وأصبح مرج ابن عامر الذهبى باهتاً يستعد لموسم خريفى آت.

تسللت بشقاوةِ الأطفال خلسةً من منزلنا لأزور الخالة «عوف» فقد اشتقت إليها كثيراً... أجلستني بجانبها في بيتها الطينى القديم... ورحت أجول بنظرى حتى وقع على قنديل زيتى قديم معلق على واجهة البيت...، وبعفويةِ الأطفال سألتها : خالتى «عوف» من أين لك هذا القنديل؟ ردت متنهدةً :..إنه قنديل قديم حملته مع جهاز عرسى والذى كان سيتم في تلك الليلة التى أخرجنا فيها الإسرائيليون من بيتنا من عكا... وها أنا أضيء هذا القنديل كل ليلة... انتظر حتى الصباح لقاء الأهل والأحبة.

الزمن لا يتوقف عند الحدث والخطب ولا يأبه بفرح الناس أو حزنهم فقد أدار ظهره لعوف وجعلها تعيش سنين عمرها تنتظر حلمها بلقاء أهلها واستعادةِ بيتها المسلوب الذى تنفست فيه نسيم البحر وهى طفلة... ولكن تبدد الحلم وسط انهيار البيت الطينى القديم المتآكل بصاروخ إسرائيلى ذكى عبر المخيم بعد نصف قرن من عذابات التشرد والحرمان... استصرخت «عوف» الأخ والأخت فلا مجيب غير صدى الصوت . لقد تبدد الحلم وسط حطام البيت والأشلاء.. ولم يبق فوق الركام سوى السوار الفضى والقنديل العكى القديم.

آمنة الكيلانى

20

The oil lamp

In my memory stays the picture of the Palestinian girl called Awf, wearing her red and green dress, with her tight red belt wrapped round her thin waist, looking like a rose at the beginning of its life. I still remember her pure white scarf covering her red, tanned face. There in her eyes I still read how brave and sharp she was. Her black hair escaped on to her face as she arranged her white scarf round her mouth, feeling shy in front of the harvesters whose sickles were cutting the heads of the wheat.

Awf was not the only one gathering wheat in Marj Ibn Aamer: she was with a lot of girls of the same age or a bit older. Marj Ibn Aamer is that plain that stretches to the horizon between Nazareth and Haifa, a heaven on earth and a secure place for people who are looking for a place to make a living, specially for people forced to leave their homeland through no fault of their own.

I did like Awf, liked Marj Ibn A'mer, the golden wheat heads dancing on the mild sea air in the evening. I liked the songs of the harvesters, so I was always to Awf, helping her gather the wheat that fell from her hands and the hands of other harvesters. Then we used to gather the wheat in a big bag, take it home and return the next day to fill it up again.

Unlike her female friends, she had no dreams to get married or have sons or daughters. She did not talk to the men who worked with us and she did not sing the harvest songs with the other girls. When I focused on her eyes, I could see how her pride was wounded. When I looked at her face, I felt a sadness. Her face was like a volcano – there could be an explosion at any moment. She talked very little; her silence gave her message. When we had food, she used to sit next to a tree, with her mind somewhere else, playing with her silver bangle. Tears used to fall down her cheeks; she swept them away quickly so no-one should see them, but I used to look at her and wonder why she was crying.

The harvest season was over, the wheat piled on a cart with four horses, and autumn came to the golden Marj Ibn Aamer. An active young child, I escaped from our house to visit Aunt Awf, because I missed her a lot. She told me to sit down beside her in her old mud house; I looked around the house and saw that old oil lamp hanging in front of the house. In my childish innocence, I asked her, "Aunt, where did you get this lamp from?"

Then, with a deep sigh, she told me: "This old light is one of the things that I was given for my wedding, which was supposed to take place that night when the Israelis forced us out of our home in Akka. And since that time, I always put on this light, waiting till I can meet my dear family and friends in the morning."

Time will never stop for any incident, it does not care for the happiness or sadness of people. Time turned its back to Awf, made her wait for all these years for nothing, for her dream of meeting her family and returning to the house which was next to the sea. But that dream is no longer alive; after fifty long years of living in shelters and poverty, her old mud house in the camp collapsed to the ground, hit by a missile. That day Awf screamed, yelled for help, called for her sisters and brothers, but she heard nothing but the echo of her screams. That dream faded among the ruins and wreckage. Nothing was left but that silver bracelet and that old Akka–made lamp.

Amneh Alkelane

21

التى فقدت ثقتها بعالم منحاز للظلم ولجأت إلى الحجر الأصم ليرفع صوتها.

وأذكر أيضا كيف عارض والدى وبشدة الذهاب لرؤية بيتنا فى البقعة بعد أن أصبحت القدس الغربية مفتوحة للمقدسيين. وكان لزيارة أخى الأصغر من الكويت فى صيف 1969 أن رضخ والدى لتوسلات أخى أن نذهب جميعنا لزيارة البقعة.

جلس والدى على يمينى فى المقعد الأمامى وكان صامتا طيلة الوقت ولكن الدم كان يحتقن فى وجه ونحن نقترب من شوارع البقعة، وحين أوقفت السيارة مقابل بيتنا، لم ينزل والدى من مقعده بل نظر إلى العمارة ولاحظ أباجور أحد الشبابيك مائلا، فتمتم بعض الكلمات ثم قال بصوت عال « ألا يستطيعون تصليح هذا الشباك؟». وأمرنى بالعودة حالا.

كان هذا السؤال من قبل والدى من أقسى ذكرياتى، وبالفعل ندمت وأخى على تعريض والدى لهذه التجربة المؤلمة. فكل ما كان يهمه (والدى) فى تلك اللحظة أن يبقى بيته الوحيد الذى تبقى له بشكل لائق حيث كان لوالدى بيت آخر فى البقعة الفوقا مؤجرا إلى موظف فى القنصلية الأمريكية ولا تزال عقود الإجارة بحوزتنا باسم Mr Phillip G Cottel لعام 1947 – 1948 ولكن هذا البيت هدم على آخرته وأقيمت مكانه عمارة سكنية بشعة. وهذه محاولة من قبل إسرائيل لطمس الوجود العربى فى القدس الغربية ولكن لا يمكنهم طمس ما فى الذاكرة.

وما يزيد الجرح إيلاما هو تصريح إسرائيل مجددا أنها دولة لليهود ما يعنى التطهير العرقى لكل من هو غير يهودى ويعنى أيضا تناقضا لادعاء إسرائيل أنها دولة لكل مواطنيها وأنها دولة ديمقراطية، ويعنى أيضا نفيا قاطعا لحق العودة.

وجاءتنا الضربة الأخيرة من قبل العاصمة واشنطن حيث ورد قرار غير ملزم من الإدارة الأمريكية ووفق عليه من قبل الكونغرس يشترط أن أى حل لمشكلة اللاجئين الفلسطينيين يجب أن يتصدى أيضا إلى جميع اللاجئين الذين أتوا إلى فلسطين من دول أخرى (أى اليهود) والذى يقدر عددهم بـ 850,000 أى أنهم أكثر من العدد المقدر للاجئين

بيت فلسطينى فى البلدة القديمة من القدس تم الاستيلاء عليه من قبل اسرائيل على يد رئيس الوزراء الأسبق شارون

Palestinian house in old Jerusalem taken over by
Israelis (this one by ex-PM Sharon)

الفلسطينيين (750,000). وإذا طبق هذا القرار فى أى حل مستقبلى فسيكون الفلسطينيون إحصائيا وماليا مدينون إلى إسرائيل أو بأحسن الأحوال لا دائن ولا مدين.

وسلام على السلام

نهلة عسلى

22

لماذا لم يصلحوا الأبجور؟

كلما زرت بيتنا فى البقعة/القدس الغربية، أوقف سيارتى مقابل العمارة التى بناها والدى فى عقد الثلاثينيات وهى تحمل اليوم رقم «17» فى شارع «هماجيد» وهى إحدى أربع عمارات تحمل طابع العمارة العربية والذى يميزها عن عمارات الشقق (علب الكبريت) التى أضافتها إسرائيل بعد 1948 فى الفسحة المفتوحة بين بيتنا وصف طويل من بيوت عائلة النمرى.

وأتساءل ، كيف ناموا فى أسرتنا، كيف عبثوا بأغراضنا، كيف استعملوا أوانى مطبخنا وجلسوا على مائدة الطعام المطلة على الحديقة الخلفية وشجرة التوت الباسقة. على المرء أن يكون مجردا من الإحساس لتحمل مثل هذه التجربة. أم أن اضطهاد اليهود ومن قبل طرف آخر يعطيهم المبررات أن يجتثوا شعبا كاملا من أرضه وأملاكه ليوفروا لأنفسهم وطنا. يقول المثل « خطآن لا يؤديان إلى الصواب» وخاصة أننا نحن الفلسطينيون لم نكن طرفا فى المسألة اليهودية بل كنا المتلقين لتبعاتها.

وتكرر والدتى (رحمها الله) كيف جرى بينها وبين والدى (رحمه الله) جدل طويل حول كمية الملابس التى ستأخذها فى الترحال إلى دمشق مع أطفالها الخمسة أثر مذبحة دير ياسين حيث قرر والدى أن نذهب برفقة والدتى للإقامة فى دمشق (والدتى من أصل سورى) عند عائلة والدتى إلى أن تهدأ الأمور فى فلسطين، وكان والدى يتحدث عن أسبوعين أو شهر على الأكثر ولا حاجة لملابس شتوية، ولكن والدتى أصّرت على أخذ قطعة صوفية لكل منا لأن دمشق قد تكون باردة فى المساء. مضى الآن ستون عاما ونحن ننتظر تلك العودة لبيتنا الجميل. عدنا بعد سنتين لنجد والدى بعد أن كان مالكا لعمارة يعيش فى نصف بيت مستأجر فى رأس العامود فى القدس الشرقية دون ماء أو كهرباء وبأقل ما يمكن من الأثاث مما تطلب من والدى موهبة الخلق والإبداع لتوفير أقل متطلبات العيش الكريم فى هذا البيت. لقد تذوقنا قساوة اللجوء بالرغم من أننا لم نسجل كلاجئين حيث أن والدى رفض لوالدتى أن تذهب إلى مكاتب تسجيل اللاجئين فى دمشق وهكذا لم تدخل أفراد عائلتى فى سجلات وكالة غوث وتشغيل اللاجئين (UNRWA) .

ما بين عامى 1948-1967 أكملنا نحن الخمسة أبناء تعليمنا الثانوى والجامعى، وكانت قناعة والدى أن لا أحد يمكنه أن يسلبنا العلم والمعرفة كما سلب أرضنا وأملاكنا، هذه كانت أيضا قناعة العديد من الفلسطينيين الذين أولوا العلم قيمة عالية بالرغم من محدودية دخلهم.

كنت أشعر بالحزن العميق حيث شاهدت أطفال وطلبة المدارس يرمون بحقائبهم وينضمون إلى المظاهرات فى الانتفاضة الأولى، ليس بسبب معارضتى للمقاومة ولكن حزنت على أجيالنا اليافعة

23

كثيرا ما حاولت مسك القلم لوضع أفكارى على الورق ولكنى فشلت، فقط بمناسبة الذكرى الستين لنكبتنا فى فلسطين -1948 -2008 ومقاربتى السبعين من العمر قررت كتابة هذه الكلمة تعبيرا عما يجول فى خاطرى من أفكار اليقظة، من التأملات، من الاعتراضات ومن الغضب المكبوت وكلما وجدت نفسى فى موقف أتحدث فيه للآخرين وخاصة الأجانب عن مواقف شخصية عايشتها حول مأساتنا كفلسطينيين، يحثنى الجميع على الكتابة وخاصة أن جيلنا الذى كان واعيا نوعا ما وقت النكبة بدأ يضمحل، « فالموت لا يبقى على أحد».

هذا السباق مع الزمن يعيد إلى ذاكرتى خبرا قصيرا فى جريدة أميركية بهذا العنوان « سباق مع الزمن» يذكر أن عددا من اليهود ومجموعة من الصهاينة ينتقدون بعض مكاتب المحامين فى الولايات المتحدة لإهمالهم وعدم كفاءتهم فى متابعة قضايا التعويض للناجين من المحرقة (الهولوكوست) والذين هم فى الثمانين من العمر حيث أنه إذا لم يتلقوا تعويضهم الآن فسيكون الوقت متأخرا كثيرا. فى لحظة قراءة هذا الخبر.

جال فى عقلى هذه الخواطر والأسئلة التى لم أفصح بها إلى رفاق السفر معى فى السيارة:-

• أنا أيضا ضحية ولكن غير معترف بى كضحية.
• ليس لدى المال أو المجموعات الضاغطة لتمثل قضيتى.
• من يجرؤ على التحدث عن حق الفلسطينيين فى العودة أو التعويض؟

لا يوجد أى اعتراف من جانب المعتدى (إسرائيل) أن هناك ضررا وظلما تاريخيا وقع على الفلسطينيين « يعيش العدو فى الإنكار ونعيش نحن المرارة بينما تستمر المعاناة ويغمض العالم عينيه».

Why can't they fix the shutters?

It has been such a long time since I wanted to put my thoughts on paper but failed to hold the pen. Had my brain been a computer and I gave it a print order, I would have filled pages of reverie, reflections, protests, stifled anger; you name it. It is only the approaching commemoration of the 60th anniversary of our Nakba and my coming of nearly 70 years of age that gave the spark. It is either now or never.

I often find myself in a situation where I have to give a speech or relate a personal encounter in relation to our predicament as Palestinians, and I almost always receive the comment that I should write these experiences down especially that our generation – those who were grown enough to remember Palestine pre 1948 – is dwindling. Death and old age spare nobody. And this hard fact reminds me of a short news item that I read in an American newspaper while sitting in a car during one of the speaking tours that I did back in 1998 which read under the very appropriate title "Race against Time" that a number of Jewish and Zionist groups are protesting the inefficiency and negligence of some law firms who are following up on the restitutions of survivors of the holocaust who were then in their late seventies or eighties and that if they were not paid now, it would be "too late". There and then, I had my brain working and in silence although I had company in the car:

* I am a victim as well, but not so vocally recognized.
* I lack the money or support groups to pay a law firm to present my case.
* Who dares to talk about the Palestinian right of return or restitution?

There is no acknowledgement on the victimizer's side that there has been a wrong-doing or historical injustice inflicted against the Palestinians. The enemy lives in denial and we live in bitterness while the suffering goes on, and the world wears its blinkers.

Whenever for some reason or another I visit our house in Baqaa, West Jerusalem, I park my car opposite the building that my father built in the 30s on what they call now Har Magied Street. It is one of four buildings in a row. Our house in particular has the aspects of architecture that distinguishes it as an Arab house, not like the ugly match box apartment buildings that were built after 1948 in the open space between our house and another row of lovely houses that belong to the Nammari Jerusalemite family.

I often wonder how the first comers who occupied or were allocated our house could sleep in our beds, use our kitchen pots and wares, dig into our drawers, eat at our dining table enjoying the view of our back garden with its huge berry tree. One has to be very hard-hearted to endure such an experience. Or is it the rationalization that the Jews were persecuted and they need a haven that justified the dispossession and uprooting of one people to provide space for another? Two wrongs do not make one right! Especially as we, the Palestinians, were not party to the whole Jewish question in Europe; We just happened to be at the receiving end.

My mother (God bless her soul) keeps repeating an argument she had with my father (God bless his soul) when back in late April 1948 after the heinous massacre of Deir Yassin, and after a bullet went through the balcony door of my parents' bedroom and ended in the bottom drawer of the dresser, my father decided to send us all – mother and five kids – to Damascus to stay with my maternal grandmother until things settled down. Mother was packing a couple of suitcases and she was adding some woollen sweaters when my father shouted at her saying that there would be no need for woollen wear since it was going to be two or three weeks at most! Mother packed a piece for each of us saying Damascus is cold at night. Well it is now sixty years after that encounter and we have not gone back to our house in Baqaa.

Two years later we came back to join my father leaving my two elder sisters in Damascus to finish high school. After being a landlord, my father rented half a house in Ras al-Amoud: entrance from the kitchen, two bedrooms, no electricity, no running water, minimal furniture. Mother borrowed some tiles and wooden boards from the landlord who happened to be a construction contractor to make shift beds for a multipurpose room: living-dining-visitors' room daytime and bedroom at night.

Mother's creativity provided us with running water by installing a small tank with a tap over the kitchen sink; she even heated it by adding boiled water to the tank in the freezing cold winter days. These may sound boring details, but we've had our share of refugee life though we were never registered as refugees because my father did not allow my mother to register at the UNRWA offices in Damascus. To him, the status of refugee is portrayed in the queue

of destitute people waiting for their monthly rations. It was his pride that did not allow his name to be entered in the UNRWA records.

Between 1948 and 1967, we all made it through schooling and higher education. It was my parents' conviction that at least we are not going to be robbed of our education. This possibly explains why the Palestinians – inspite of their meager incomes- put great value on learning.

To me, it was very saddening when schoolchildren threw away their school bags to join the demonstrations in the first Intifada. Not that I am against resistance, but the act symbolizes that the younger generation – children and youth – lost faith in a world that is so biased, and resorted to the mute stone to speak for them.

Coming back to my father, I remember him strongly denying the very idea of going to see our house in Baqaa after 1967 when West Jerusalem became accessible to Palestinians living in East Jerusalem.

It was in the summer of 1969 when my brother, who was then working in Kuwait, came to visit us through what they called then family visit permits. Through appealing, cajoling, repeated arguments, my father finally consented and we drove to Baqaa. Sitting next to me in the front seat, my father did not utter a word but I could see the bluish blood congested in his face. As I parked the car, he remained seated, looked at the 3-storey building and noticed one of the shutters facing the road slanted sideways. He mumbled a few intangible utterances and then said aloud, "Can't they fix the shutters?" and ordered me to drive back home.

To me personally, my father's comment about the shutters was, and still is, one of the most hurtful memories, and my brother and I really regretted subjecting father to that agonizing ordeal. All that mattered to him at that moment was to have HIS only remaining house in good shape. My father owned another house in upper Bakaa which was leased to Mr Philip G Cottel, someone who worked at the USA Consulate in Jerusalem then (I wonder if he or any member of his family can attest to this), but that house was raised to the ground soon after the 1967 war, and an ugly multi-storey building stands in its place. My father never saw the house nor did he bother to see the ugly building. This, in fact, is Israel's way to obliterate our physical existence in West Jerusalem and in Palestine at large; it will never succeed in obliterating our memories. They do not take a delete order.

To add insult to injury, Israel recently came up with the idea of the pure Jewish state; the implication of which means ethnic cleansing of anybody who is not Jewish which contradicts its claim that it's a state for all its people and that it's democratic. It also negates any implementation of the right of return.

The final blow directed to us Palestinians came from Washington DC where a non-committal resolution to the administration was approved by the Congress which stipulates that any solution to the issue of the Palestinian refugees should also address the case of the Jewish refugees who came to settle in Palestine or other countries and whose number was as stated in the news item, 850,000, which in fact exceeds the number of Palestinian refugees who were forced out of their homeland in 1948 (750,000). If this is to be pursued in any future solution, we, the Palestinians, will end up owing the Jews some money or in the best of cases we'll break even. Goodbye to peace.

Nahla Assali

الــطرد من الارض

Forced off the land

من خلال السياج

أريد أن اروى لكم قصة بلدتى بيت صفافا ... قسمت هذة البلدة الى قسمين بعد هدنه عام 1948 ، قسم من البلدة بمن بقى فيه وقع فى حدود ما صار يعرف بعد الحرب بإسرائيل والجزء الآخر تحت الحكم الأردن. عائلة أمى وإخوتها كانوا تعيش تحت سيطرة إسرائيل وأمى مع أبى كانت تعيش تحت حكم الأردن.

بلدتنا فصلت بسياج حيث لم يكن يسمح للناس على الجانبين من الحديث مع بعضهم من خلال السياج إلا فى حالات الوفاة او الزواج، كان الأقارب فى الطرفين يقفون بجانب السياج ويتكلموا مع بعضهم وما عدا ذلك كان ممنوع ومن يخالف يعتقل ويضع بالسجن من قبل الطرفين سواء الأردنيون او الإسرائيليون.

أنا أتذكر حين كان عمرى 5 سنوات كان لنا جارة كبيرة فى السن وكان لديها أخ فى الجانب الإسرائيلى من السياج أراد أن يعطيها بعض الطعام من خلال فتحة صغيرة فى السياج استخدمه الناس لتبادل الأغراض وفى لحظة التبادل أتى شرطى إسرائيلى، حاولت جارتنا سحب يدها على

عجل لتهرب، جرحت يدها وبدأت تنزف دما.

وأذكر أيضا أن أمى أخبرتنى انه لم يكن مسموح لهم حتى تحضير الطعام الا بقدر محدود وكان يجب أن يحصلوا على تصريح مسبق من الجيش الأردنى فى حال أرادوا إحضار المواد التموينية الى بيت صفافا وان يذكروا الكميات التى يريدون شراؤها وهذا كان شىء صعب جدا.

ولا زالت أذكر خالتى التى كانت فى الجانب الإسرائيلى من السياج وكانت تريد أن تتزوج من قريب لها كان فى الجانب الأردنى مما استدعى تهريبها عبر الحدود بطريقة صعبة وقد ترتب على ذلك فقدانها للهوية الإسرائيلية ولم يسمح لها العودة مرة أخرى ... هذة القصة عن بيت صفافا.

أود أن أخبركم قصة عن صديق كان زميل لى فى جامعة بير زيت هو أصلا من مدينة يافا ويعيش الآن فى مخيم جنين، وكان يحكى لنا دائما عن بيته فى يافا. وكيف كان على الدوام يذهب الى يافا قبل أن يمنع المواطنين من زيارة منازلهم هناك فى فترة السبعينات .... كان يقول انه كان يذهب الى منزله فى يافا ويقرع الجرس ويهرب، هذا كان يذكرنى بالفلسطينيين الذين كانوا يزورون بيوتهم التى استولى عليها الإسرائيليون وسكنوها ...

هيام عليان

Through the fence

elderly lady took her hand away quickly and started to run away. Her hand started to bleed.

Later, my mother told me that the people from Beit Safafa from the Jordanian side were not even allowed foodstuffs unless they had been specified. People had to apply for the permit for foodstuffs and write down

I want to tell you about my village called Beit Safafa. It was divided into two parts after the ceasefire in 1948. Some of the village and the people who lived in it came into the part that came to be called Israel, and the other part was with Jordan. My mother's family were living under Israeli control but my mother and my father living under the Jordanians.

There was a sort of a fence that divided the village. People were allowed to talk through the fence if someone had died or got married but it was forbidden at all other times. If they saw people speaking with each other across the fence then they would put them in prison, whether they were on the Jordanian or Israeli side.

I remember when I was 5 years old, we had a neighbour who was an elderly woman who had a brother that was living on the Israeli side. Her brother wanted to pass a gift of foodstuffs to her. There was a small hole in the fence where they wanted to exchange these things. When he started to pass them over, the Israeli military patrol came. The

the type of foodstuffs and the quantities they wanted to buy. This was very difficult.

My auntie was on the Israeli side and she was getting married to someone from the Jordanian side and they had to smuggle her through – it was very difficult. My auntie had an Israeli identity and so marrying someone from the Jordanian side meant that she would have to lose her Israeli identity. This is just one of many stories from Beit Safafa.

I want to tell you about a friend of mine from Jaffa. He was studying at Bir Zeit University at the same time as me. He is living now in the Jenin Refugee Camp. He was always telling me about his house in Jaffa, which they used to go and visit. Until the 70s, people were not prevented from going back to visit Jaffa. He would go to his house in Jaffa and have to ring the bell and run away. Lots of Palestinians used to go back to their houses and find that Jewish people were living in them.

Hiyam Elayyan

المرة تلو المرة

1948 عندما كان والدى شابا ومتزوجا حديثا وكان لهم طفل عمره عام ونصف، فى تلك الفترة كان والدى تاجر مواشى وكان له ارض يزرعها فى منطقة قريبة من حيفا تسمى اللجون بالقرب من سجن مجدو حاليا.

عندما بدأت الحرب كان موسم الحصاد قام الجيش الإسرائيلى وبإحراق محصولنا، هرب والدى ووالدى وأخى الصغير وابن عمه الذى قتل أثناء الحرب.

كانت اقرب منطقة على اللجون هى مدينة جنين وساروا مشيا على الأقدام لمسافة 35 كم، استأجر والدى بيتا فى جنين كان يستخدم للحيوانات، حيث وولدت أنا وثلاثة شقيقات.

أخبرتى أمى أن والدى بدأ يعمل فى تجارة الحيوانات، لم يشأ والدى أن يسكن المخيم وكان يرفض تسمية لاجئ، لكن درسنا جميعا فى مدارس الوكالة وبقينا نسكن فى مدينة جنين حتى عام 1967 وكان هناك صعوبة لدى والدى فى تربيتنا والحصول على المال الكافى، ولم يبنى لنا بيت كان لديه أمل فى العودة الى بلده وعشنا طول الفترة فى بيوت مستأجرة.

فى عام 1967 فى الخامس من حزيران قامت الحرب وكان عمرى 5 سنوات بكيت كثيرا ... بكيت من الحرب ولان حلم والدى بالعودة قد تلاشى الى الأبد.

والدى الذى اشترى لى حذاء جديد وفستان جديد اشترى لأنى حصلت على الدرجة الاولى فى صفى، بكيت لأنى تركت هذه الأشياء وهربت مع أسرتى الى الأردن والدى كان قلقا بان يتكرر ما حصل فى عام 1948.

أخى الكبير رفض أن يهرب معنا لاعتقاده انه يجب أن يبقى فى بلده وأرضه وعندما قطعنا مسافة حوالى 30 كم طلبنا من والدى أن نعود مرة ثانية لنحضر أخى، عدت مع أختى الكبرى ومع عمى وأخذناه معنا، بعد ثلاث أيام من المسير وصلنا الى منطقة تسمى الكرامة فى الأردن.

لقد شعرت بالإعياء الشديد والمرض نتيجة المشى الطويل وكان أبى مضطرا لحملى، عند وصولنا الأردن مكثنا عند خالى وعمى اللذان هاجرا مع عائلاتهم من فلسطين عام 1948.

عانينا كثيرا لان الحياة فى الأردن كانت سيئة جدا، لذلك طلبنا من والدى أن يعود بنا الى فلسطين أو الضفة الغربية، عدنا بواسطة الصليب الأحمر عدنا الى البيت الذى كنا نستأجره وجدنا كل المحتويات قد أتلفت ونهبت ودمرت وكان أبى يملك 200 رأس من الماشية لم نجد أى منها وعاد أبى من الصفر حتى كبرنا وتعلمنا بالجامعات.

التهجير الثالث كان عندما تزوجت وسكنت فى قرية على حدود 1948 داخل الضفة الغربية حيث قام الإسرائيليون بمصادرة ارض زوجى وارض حوالى 64 دونم بحجة أنها قريبة من المستوطنة مما أدى الى إصابة زوجى بمرض السكرى.

شعرت بان أولادى سيعيشون لاجئين كما عشت، بسبب مصادرة هذه الأراضى وللأسف لازلت أتشرد لأننى الآن لا أستطيع أن ادخل الى بيتى بدون تصريح تصدره السلطات الإسرائيلية، على مدخل بلدتنا توجد بوابة حديدية مكهربة يحرسها جنود إسرائيليون لا يستطيع أحد الدخول عبرها بدون التصريح.

آمنة الكيلانى

30

Again and again

we studied at the refugee schools [UN schools], and we continued living in the Jenin area, until 1967. My father had difficulty raising us, particularly financially. He never attempted to build a house because he had always hoped to return to his home and so we always lived in rented houses.

On 5th June 1967, we had the Six Day War between Israel and the Arab World. I was 10 years old and when the war started I cried a lot. I cried because of the war and because my father had lost his dream of returning to the place he came from.

He bought me shoes and a dress because I was the first in my class. I left these things in the house and we had to run away towards Jordan because my father was afraid that the same would happen to us as happened in 1948.

My big brother did not run away because he believed that he must die in his own country. After we had walked for 30km we asked our father to go back and get our brother. I came back with my other sister and my uncle and we took him with us. We arrived three days later at a place called Al Karameh in Jordan. I became sick because walking had affected my feet and my father had to carry me once we arrived. When we reached Jordan my two uncles were waiting for us there; they had fled their homes and been living there since 1948.

We cried lots because living in Jordan was very bad. We asked our father if we could go back to Palestine or the West Bank and we came back with the Red Cross. When we returned to the house that we rented we saw that all of our stuff had been demolished or stolen and my father had had lost all 200 of his sheep. We had to start life again from zero until we grew up and all went to university.

We were made refugees again when I got married and lived in a village on the 1948 borders, inside the West Bank. The Israelis confiscated our land, about 64 dunams, because it was near to the settlements. My husband developed diabetes because of the confiscation of the land.

I think that my children will also be refugees because of the confiscation of land.

Amneh Alkilani

In 1948, when my father was a young man and my mother was a young woman, they were newly married and had an only son. My brother was then one and a half years old. My father was a sheep seller and he had land in a place near Haifa called Al Lajun, very near where Majido prison is now. He used to cultivate the land.

When the 1948 war took place, it was harvest time and the Israeli army burned all of their crops. My father, mother, little brother and one cousin ran away; the cousin was killed.

The closest area to the Lajun area was the Jenin area and they walked the whole distance, for 35 km. My father rented a small room that used to be used for animals. I was one year old at that time but my mother has told me that my father started working selling animals. I had three other sisters.

We never lived in a refugee camp because my father was always angry with the word 'refugee'. However,

أين طفلتي؟

أود أن اروى قصة حماتى التى عاشت كطفله يتيمة بعد موت والدتها وهى فى التاسعة من عمرها حيث تركت المدرسة لكى ترعى أشقائها، الحياة كانت صعبة جدا قبل حرب 1967 كانت تمشى مسافة طويلة لتجلب الماء والخشب لعمل النار لتحضير الطعام لأشقائها.

حين كبرت وتزوجت كان زوجها يعمل فى الأردن.

مع بداية حرب حزيران عام 1967 هرب العديد من الناس من ابوديس والعيزرية وتوجهوا الى الأردن .

على الحدود الأردنية حدث زحام شديد وتدافع الناس فى محاولة قطع الجسر الخشبى على النهر، لم تستطع حماتى الصمود فسقطت طفلتها من يدها ولم تستطيع العثور عليها فى الزحام لتترك الطفلة لتعيش يتيمة بعيدا عن العائلة، كان شعور حماتى بالذنب كبير جداً على اعتبار أنها عاشت يتيمة وطفلتها اليوم ستعيش نفس الظرف.

عندما وصلت الى الأردن طلبت من كل من كان معها البحث عن طفلتها، بدأ الجميع بالبحث دون جدوى واعتقدوا أنها توفيت، قبل أن يتمكنوا من العثور على الطفلة.

واجهت حماتى مشاكل كثيرة وصعوبات فى العودة الى الضفة الغربية، ولم تكن طريق العودة آمنة لكنها فى النهاية استطاعت أن تعود الى ابوديس.

رنا فرعون

32

Where is my daughter?

I'd like to talk about my mother in-law's story. When she was a child, she was orphaned; her mother died when she was nine years old. She left school in order to look after her sisters and brothers. Life was very difficult before the war in 1967; she used to walk a long distance to bring water and wood and make fire and bring food for her brothers and sisters.

When she grew up and got married, her husband used to work in Jordan.

In 1967, when the war started, people started to run away from Abu Dis and Aizariyeh go to Jordan.
At the borders, everyone was pushing and shoving each other. Her daughter fell over and became separated from her, and people were pushing each other. She went with them, terrified. She remembered her daughter, and what guilt she felt as she herself was raised as an orphan.

She went back to find her daughter and was separated from her family. When she reached Jordan she found them at last, and discovered that everyone had been searching for her, and everyone thought that she had died.

She found many problems and difficulties in returning to where she lived in the West Bank. But she managed to get back to Abu Dis.

Rana Faraon

33

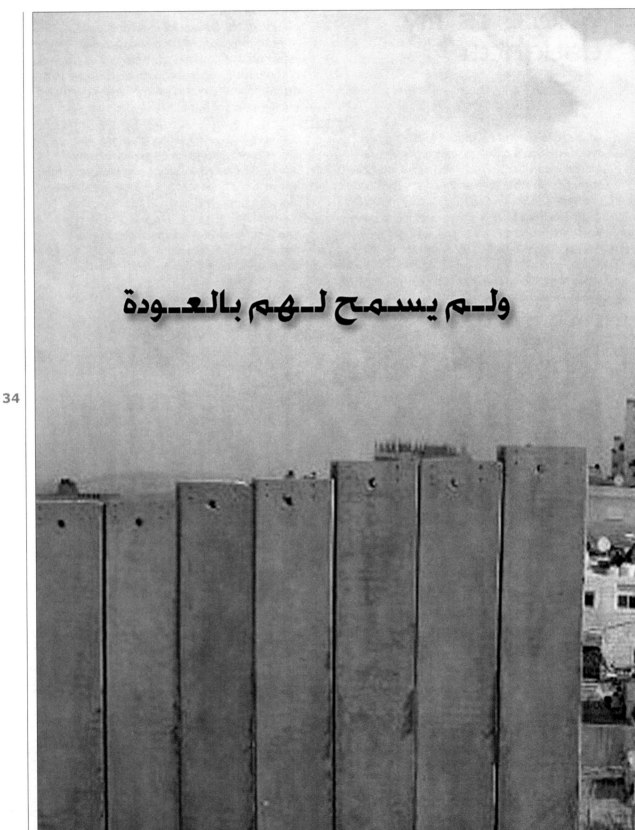

ولــم يســمح لـهـم بالعــودة

And not allowed back

صراع من اجل العودة

غادرت العائلةُ الى الكويت فى العام 1960 طلبا للرزق وتحسين الوضع الاقتصادى على نية العودة الى الوطن.

العائلةُ مكونةٌ من 8 أشخاص، عندما وقعت حرب حزيران 1967 منع من كانوا خارج الوطن من العودة نهائيا حرموا من الوطن الذى ضاع ما تبقى منه فى هذه الحرب.

كبر الأولاد وبدأوا بشق طريقهم فى الحياة، تزوج الشقيقان الكبيران من فتاتين من ابوديس وكونهن مكثن مدةً طويلةً خارج الوطن منعن من الحضور ثانيةً الى فلسطين إلا بتصريح زيارةٍ ولمدةِ شهرين فقط من يخالف يطرد بأمر عسكرى ما زلت اذكر كيف طردت إحداهن فى الصباح الباكر والثلوج تغطى المنطقة نقلت فى جيب عسكرى إسرائيلى أوصلها الحدود الأردنية حيث كانت حامل فمات جنينها فور وصولها الكويت.

تفرق شمل العائلة، ذهب الأبناء الى أمريكا وتوفى العم أبو يوسف ومنعت جنازته من العبور الى فلسطين لتدفن فيها رغم وصيته بذلك.

بعد حرب الخليج الاولى خرج من تبقى من العائلة الى الأردن، بعد اتفاق أوسلو سمح لبعض من فقدوا هوياتهم بالعودة، بقيت الحاجةُ أم يوسف وحيدةً فى الأردن ليس لها احد يرعاها ابنها الذى عاد الى ابوديس تقديم طلب جمع شمل لها فى العام 1993 لكنه لم ينجح.

كان لمرض ابنها المقيم فى ابوديس وإشرافه على الموت دوراً كبيراً فى عودتها حيث تدخل الصليب الأحمر ونجح فى استصدار تصريح زيارة لها لتودع ابنها الوداع الأخير رحل الابن عن الدنيا ورفضت هى المغادرة وبقيت فى ابوديس بلا إقامةٍ أو هوية، مهددةً بالطرد فى أى لحظة، أصبحت حبيسة البيت لم تستطع الخروج منه، لا يمكنها الذهاب للصلاة فى المسجد الأقصى ولا حتى الذهاب الى المستشفى اذا ما مرضت، خاصة بعد إقامة الجدار استمر ابنها الثانى فى محاولاته للحصول على هوية لامه، وفى شتاء 2008 حصلت الحاجةُ صفية على هويةٍ وهى تبلغ من العمر 88 سنة.

قالت لى أنهم أعطوها الهوية فقط من اجل أن يسلمها ابنها بعد وفاتها، لتنظيم إجراءات دفنها.

اغتربوا للبحث عن الرزق وأصبحوا لاجئين ولهم وطن، حلموا لكنهم رحلوا قبل أن يحققوا الحلم الذى طال انتظارهم له وتفرقوا فى أنحاء الأرض –فأى جمع شمل هذا؟ –ماذا أرادت الحجةُ صفية من هويتها التى حصلت عليها. بقيت اثنان وأربعون عام وهى حبيسةُ سريرها لا تغادره إلا لقضاء حاجة.

نجاح عياد

Struggle to return

The family left for Kuwait in 1960, in search of a livelihood and an improvement in their economic condition. They intended to return to the land they left.

The family consisted of eight people. When the 1967 war broke out, the people who were outside Palestine were completely forbidden to return. They were deprived of their nation which lost what remained of it in this war.

The children grew up and embarked on their difficult paths in life. The older two boys married two girls from Abu Dis who had been out of the country a long time and now were forbidden from returning unless they obtained a visit permit for just two months. Anyone who stayed longer than that period would be expelled by military order.

I still remember how they expelled one of them in the early morning when snow covered the region. A military jeep took them to the Jordanian border. when one of the women was pregnant. She lost the baby on the way to Kuwait.

The family unit was split up. The sons went to America and Uncle Abu Yusuf died. The funeral party was prevented from crossing into Palestine to bury him, which is what he had wanted.

After the first Gulf War, what remained of the family fled to Jordan and after the Oslo Accords they were able to return to Palestine.

Only Hajeh Um Yusuf remained in Jordan; there was no one with her to look after her. Her son who had returned to Abu Dis tried to submit an application for the reunion in 1993 but the son became ill and it was thought that he would die. The Red Cross intervened and after several attempts, they agreed that the should mother be allowed to enter to say her final goodbye to her son.

Her son died and she remained in Abu Dis without papers, under threat of expulsion at any moment. She was not able to go to pray in the Al Aqsa mosque nor was she even allowed to go to the hospital when she got ill, especially after the construction of the Separation Wall. Her second son continued to try and obtain an ID for his mother in the winter of 2008. She finally obtained her ID when she was 88 years old.

She told me "They gave me the ID just in time to get permission to be buried."

Najah Ayyad

حمدا لله أنها نسيتها

حدثتني أمي أنه قبل حرب 1967 قررت عائلتنا أن تسافر الى الخارج في رحلة، وأنها ذهبت لاستصدار جواز سفر ولم تتذكر حمل صورها الشخصية الضرورية لعمل جواز السفر معها مما اضطرها للرجوع الى البيت لتحضر الصور، كان ذلك في صبيحة يوم الخامس من حزيران حيث بدأت العمليات العسكرية لحرب حزيران 1967، وقد حمدت أمي فيما بعد أنها نسيت الصور لان هناك كثير من الناس بدأوا بالهرب وان الكثير من الناس الذين كانوا خارج الوطن لم يتمكنوا من العودة بعد الحرب ولكن قليلون من استطاعوا العودة.

بعد الاحتلال 1967 بدأ الإسرائيليون عملية إحصاء للسكان في القدس وسلموا كل من تواجد في المدينة هويات زرقاء، فيما حصل سكان مناطق الضفة الغربية هويات برتقالية، كان الجميع يعتقد بأن سكان القدس محظوظين بحصولنا على هوية القدس، ولكن هذا غير صحيح لأننا ندفع ضرائب كثيرة للإسرائيليين وبالقوة والإكراه.

حيث تستخدم إسرائيل سياسة الضرائب المرتفعة كمحاولة لتقليل عدد السكان العرب في القدس وتهجير ما أمكن منهم، في هذه السنة تم سحب هويات 4,000 فلسطيني من سكان القدس، جميعهم من مواليد القدس ولهم الحق في العيش فيها.

ونحن الآن في نناضل من اجل الحفاظ على هوية القدس والبقاء في المدينة المحتلة،، لان الإسرائيليون ينتظرون على الدوام أي مبرر من اجل سحب الهوية المقدسية، تتم عملية إحصائنا بشكل دوري في القدس.

أود أن اروي قصة في عائلتي هذه ليست قصة شخصية ولكن قصة كل الناس في القدس لدى شقيقتان متزوجتان من رجلان في غزة، حسب القوانين الإسرائيلية فلا يحق لأخواتي العيش خارج مدينة القدس ولا يحق لأزواجهن من غزة العيش في القدس، لا تستطعن ترك هويتهن ولا يستطعن ترك أزواجهن وهن الآن في حيرة من أمرهن.

تعيش أخواتي وبناتهن اليوم في القدس وليس لديهم الحق في العيش في غزة اما الأزواج فهم في غزة وليس لديهم إمكانية الخرج منها والعيش مع عائلاتهم في القدس، تلقى العائلة مرة واحدة في السنة عندما تسمح إسرائيل للرجال بالحصول على تصريح لان التصريح يدفع له الكثير من النقود وخاصة أهل غزة فالحصول اليوم على تصريح شبه مستحيل.

أنا اسكن في العيزرية وهذا ممنوع حسب القوانين الإحتلاليه لان العيزرية تعتبر خارج نطاق حدود بلدية

القدس الإسرائيلية أي في الضفة الغربية وأنا أحمل هوية القدس ولا يسمح لي بالعيش في الضفة ....لا زلنا نعيش كما نريد نحن وليس كما يريدون هم، حسب قوانينهم حامل هوية القدس لا يستطيع أن يسكن الضفة وإن فعل يفقد هويته ولا يستطيع رؤية أهله.

بينما الإسرائيلي الذي يحمل الهوية الإسرائيلية يسمح له بالعيش في الضفة الغربية.

كذلك قصة عمتي هذه القصة تحصل في كل مكان عمتي عمرها سبعين عاما ذهبت الى أمريكا لزيارة أولادها الذين يعيشون هناك هروبا من الضغط الموجود في المناطق المحتلة وفجأة سحب الإسرائيليون هويتها المقدسية، ولدت عمتي في باب العامود في القدس وعاشت ساكنين في القدس ورجعت الى فلسطين بفيزا لزيارة القدس ولمدة عشرة أيام وهي لا تملك غرين كارد في أمريكا.

سمر سحار

38

Thank God she forgot it

My mother told me that before the 1967 war, they were planning to go on holiday and my mother went to get her passport. However, she had forgotten the photo so she came back to the house to get it.

Thank God that she had forgotten the the photo. Many people were frightened and ran away when war broke out, others were out of the country or on holiday; they thought that they were going to come back the next week or the week after but they never did. Only a few were able to return so thank God that she is in this country.

After counting the population that had remained in Jerusalem, the Israelis gave us blue IDs. This ID is different to the Palestinian and West Bank identity cards, because we are considered to be people of Jerusalem. Some people from the West Bank think that we are lucky because we have Jerusalem identity cards but this is not true. We pay lots and lots of taxes to the Israelis and we are forced to pay these taxes.

Through taxes, they are trying to reduce the number of people in Jerusalem. This year, four thousand people who live in Jerusalem have had their blue IDs taken away from them. They were born in Jerusalem; they should be able to live there. For us, we are in a struggle to preserve our Jerusalem identity. It is a struggle that continues every day. The Israelis watch over everything we do just to find an excuse to take away our Jerusalem identity. We are searched even when we are in Jerusalem.

I want to tell you a story from my own family. This is not really a personal story but is the story of all of the people in Jerusalem.

I have two sisters married to men in Gaza. In order to keep their identity cards, my sisters cannot live with their husbands. My sisters have to make a choice – either their husbands or their identity cards. My sisters and my nieces are living in Jerusalem because they were Jerusalem-born and Israel says they have no right to be in Gaza. The husbands and fathers are in Gaza and they cannot come out of Gaza. So the families see each other just once

a year, if the Israelis decide to give them permits to come. Even if they give permission, it is very expensive for Gaza people – it is nearly impossible.

I live in Bethany but, according to Israeli regulations, I am not allowed to, because our Jerusalem identity card means that we are not allowed to live in the West Bank. We live as we like and not as they want us to live. If a Palestinian has a Jerusalem ID, given by the Israelis, they are not able to live in the West Bank because they will lose their ID, and then they will not be able to see their family in Jerusalem.

But note that an Israeli who carries Israeli identity is able to live in the West Bank – in the settlements.

I have a story about my auntie, she is 70 years old. She went to visit her children in America because they left Palestine because of the torture and the struggles of everyday life. They thought they would make a new life in America. She went to see her children but suddenly the Israelis took her Jerusalem identity. She is Bab al-Amoud (Damascus Gate) – born and that is where all of her family have lived for ages back. She came to Palestine with a visa for ten days to visit Jerusalem. She is 70 years old and she doesn't have the Green Card in America.

Samar Sahhar

إحدى عشر عاماً

هذا صحيح الذى قالته السيدة فريدة ، اذا لم أنت تقاتل لا
احد سيقاتل عنك ، امى فعلت هذا هى عادت مع والدى
وعشرة من الأبناء الى فلسطين، وقد توفى والدى بعد عودتهم.

رفض الإسرائيليون بقاء امى فى فلسطين وقالوا لها لا أنت
كولمبية لذلك ارجعى الى كولمبيا وهى قالت لا أنا فلسطينية
وزوجى فلسطينى ولنا قرية ولنا أرض ولنا أشجار زيتون وكل
أقاربنا فى فلسطين، فقالوا لا، لا تستطيعين البقاء هنا ارجعى ...

عانت امى احد عشر عام لاستعادة هويتها، هى من هنا لا
تحتاج الى رخصة للبقاء، ولا تحتاج الى تصريح، اذا كنت
خارج انجلترا وأردت العودة لا تحتاج الى تصريح لتعود الى
منزلك.

ولكن امى قاتلت إحدى عشر عام لتسكن فى فلسطين، لم
يكن هذا سهلا مطلقا لأنها كانت تذهب لتجديد تصريح
الزيارة كل شهر، جلبت معى الملف الذى كانت تحمله كل
شهر الى الإدارة المدنية.

أنتى حصلتى على فيزا فلسطينية أو إسرائيلية أليس كذلك؟
كذلك امى فعلت هذا لمدة أحد عشر عام تذهب وتأتى ..
وكانت الأختام تعطى فقط لمدة 15 أو 17 من الشهر
تذهب لتجديد التصريح لذلك بقيت تذهب مرة بعد مرة بعد
مرة، إحدى هذه الاوراق (فى الملف) تحوى أسماء الاطفال
العشرة وكل واحد منا يجب ان يحصل على ورقة كهذه لانه
اذا اوقفنا الجنود بدونها سنعاقب .

فى هذا الملف كل شهر توقيع وتشير الى ختم بالملف وهذا
كان مكلف كذلك كل شهر كنا ندفع نقود لاحد تصريح
زيارة ....

لو لم تكن امى قوية ولم تخض معركتها من أجل حقنا فى
الوجود على ارضنا فلا اعتقد أننا من الممكن أن نكون هنا
اليوم ولكنت أعيش فى أمريكا اللاتينية.
وصلت امى الى فلسطين وقدمت طلب لم شمل للعائلة،
طلب من امى ان تأتى الى المكتب المدنى الإسرائيلى وأن
تحضر معها قائمة من الوثائق المطلوبة وفعلت.

الإسرائيليون لا يتعاملون معنا كبشر بل يرونا كمادة لهم،
وعليه كانت امى تذهب شهريا وتجلس لساعات ربما أحيانا
تذهب الساعة الثامنة صباحا فيغلقون المكتب المدنى ويقولون
لها الكابتن لم يأتى، من الممكن أن يأتى بعد الظهر، نحن لسنا
من رام الله نحن من قرية ولذلك كانت تخرج من المكتب
وتجلس فى الشارع ساعتين حتى لا تضيع فرصة تجديد
التصريح وهذا صعب جدا لها.

فى إحدى المناسبات قالت فيها امى «نعم ما هذه الحالة» ....
بهذا الوضع لن نتمكن من البقاء فى الوطن ... ذهبت امى الى

40

محامى ورفعت قضية فى المحكمة الإسرائيلية فى العام 1981
أقرت المحكمة الإسرائيلية بالسماح لوالدتى بالبقاء فى فلسطين،
وعندما ذهبت الى مكتب الإدارة المدنية قال لها الضابط
الإسرائيلى المسئول بأنه لا يمكنها البقاء، وأن هناك خطأ، فقالت
أنا أملك الوثيقة والإثباتات فأخبروها لا، هناك خطأ واستغرق
تصحيح الخطأ سبع سنوات أخرى لذلك كان هناك إحدى
عشر سنة لنحصل على إحدى عشر هوية .....

بالنسبة لى، فلدى الحق فى العيش هنا، وهذا هذا وطنى، وهذه
أرض أبى، قبل أسبوع كنا نقطف الزيتون. لا يستطيعون أخذ
أرضنا فقط لأن لديهم القوة والإسناد من كل العالم، يستطيعون
أخذ أرضى، يستطيعون أخذ معطفى ولكن لا يمكنهم قتل روحى
وذهنى أبداً.

لذلك أنا موجودة هنا الآن فى وطنى، لهذا أنا أريد أن أخدم
شعبى. امى عملت ما استطاعت. بالمناسبة لقد بدأت فى تعلم
اللغة العربية فى جمعية إنعاش الأسرة وهذه إحدى قصص
النجاح.

من كلمة القتها إسبرنزا فى جمعية إنعاش الأسرة

Eleven years

That's right, what Miss Foreda said, that if you don't fight, no one will do it for you. My mother did it, she came back with my father. We are ten children, my father was dead, and she wanted to come back to her homeland. The Israelis refused her and they told her, "No, you are Colombian, so go back to Colombia", and she said "No, I am Palestinian, and my husband is Palestinian, and we have a village, and we have our land and we have our olives, and we have all our family in Palestine". They said, "No, you can't stay here, go back".

It took her eleven years to regain her ID. Legally, she's from here, she doesn't need a permit, she doesn't need permission. If you are outside of England and you go back, you don't need anything to go back to your house. But my mother fought for eleven years to stay in Palestine.

It wasn't easy at all, because she went every single month to renew to ours visitors' permits. Look at this file I have with me. Every single month she had to go an renew it. You got a visa for visiting Palestine, or Israel, right? My mother did that every month for eleven years, just going again and again, and each time they just stamped it for one month. On the 15th or the 17th of the month, they renewed the permit for her, so she had to go again and again and again and again. One of the papers that I hsve in this file is the names of the ten children. So, every one of us had to carry a sheet of paper like this, in case they stopped us and we didn't have identity cards. Look at this huge file, every single one of these is one month; and not for free. Every single month we had to buy eleven new visitors.

If she hadn't been that strong and if she hadn't put up a fight, we wouldn't be here. We would maybe be in Latin America again, or I don't know where. My mother asked for a family reunion and they told her to come to the Civil Department.

They don't see us as people, they don't see us Palestinians, as human beings. She asked them for a family reunion, so she was asked, "Okay, you have to come to the Civil Office, and bring with you the following materials" ...and they gave my mother's name. To them, my mother was an object, not a person or a human being.

So every single month she sat there. Sometimes she went at 8 o'clock in the morning, but they closed the Civil Office and told her, "The Captain hasn't come, come back in the afternoon". We are from a village, we are not from Ramallah. So she had to go out from the office and sit down in the street for 2 hours, and return, so that she did not miss the chance of the Cpatain renewing her permit.

It was very difficult for her, and then one day, mother said, "What is this state that will not allow me to come back to my homeland?" So she went to a lawyer and raised a case in the court, bringing all her children to the court.

In 1981, they told my mother, "Okay, you are allowed to stay", and my mother went to the Office. But they told her, "No, no, it was a mistake; you're not allowed to stay". So she said, "But I have the document, we have the document here", but they told her, "No, no it was a mistake", and it took her another seven years. So it took eleven years to gain our eleven IDs.

But I am a person, I have the right to be here, because this is my homeland, because this is my father's land. One week ago we were picking our olives. They can't take our land because they are strong and the world is behind them. They can take my land, they can take my coat but they can't take my spirit and my mind. Never.

And that's why I stayed here, that's why I stayed in my homeland, that's why I wanted to, to serve my people. My mother did what she was able to do. Ah, by the way, we started our Arabic lessons in In'ash al Usra, so this is one of the success stories you can see, because my sister is also doing her PhD in Harvard. It's not easy to get there.

From a talk given by Esperanza at In'ash al Usra, Ramallah

عنف الجيـــش

Army violence

عبء الأعمال المنزلية اللامنتهية، وعيناها ترنو إلى أبعد من ذلك المنزل.

حاولت أكثر من مرة العودة لاستكمال دراستها لكن في كل مرة كان يحدث ما يعرقل قرارها غير أنها بقيت عازمة على العودة للتعلم من جديد ولو بعد حين.

وتذكر هيفاء بصوت واثق كيف استطاعت في النهاية التقدم لامتحان القبول لدى وزارة التربية والتعليم واجتيازه بنجاح ليتسنى لها دراسة الثانوية العامة بعد ذلك.

لم تكن أوقاتها مليئة بالمذاكرة والدراسة بالطبع ، تقول هيفاء : « فقدت أكثر الناس سندا وعونا لي في الحياة ألا وهي أمي » تعني بذلك أن مسؤولية البيت ألقيت على عاتقها بالكامل منذ رحيل والدتها لأنها أكبر أخواتها ، فأصبحت تعمل في البيت نهارا ، وتدرس ليلا مع أنها لم تلتحق بمدرسة خاصة لتقوم بدور المعلم والتلميذ في الوقت ذاته ، ولكنها كانت أقوى من ظروفها الصعبة والمحبطة في بعض الأحيان كما تقول هي.

وتابعت هيفاء القول أن دراستها في تلك الفترة كانت من ضروب المستحيل أو العبث كما في اعتقادها ، ويزداد الوضع صعوبة خلال فترة الامتحانات العامة حيث يصاب أصغر إخوتها عمار (١١ عاما) بحجر صغير في رأسه أثناء

تواجده قرب أطفال يتراشقون بالحجارة ، مما يؤدي إلى كسر في عظم جمجمته.

يتضاعف بذلك ألم هيفاء على أخيها الصغير إضافة إلى أخويها اللذين يرقدان في المستشفى للعلاج ، ومسؤولية البيت في المقابل ، فضلا عن امتحانات الثانوية التي طالما انتظرتها ، وتصف هيفاء ذلك بقولها : « أحسست أن هذه المصيبة هي الضربة القاضية على مستقبلي الدراسي ، وأن كل الأبواب قد أغلقت في وجهي « ، وتضيف :» ولكني توكلت على الله وفي النهاية نجحت « ، وبالفعل فقد اجتازت هيفاء امتحان الثانوية العامة وبنتيجة ٧٥٪.

وتعقب هيفاء : « وأنا الآن متزوجة وعلى وشك الإنجاب وأتابع دراستي الجامعية يوميا ، رغم رعايتي لبيتي وزوجي وأولاده من زوجته المتوفاة ، فالمشوار طويل ولا زلت في بداية الطريق».

وما قصة هيفاء إلا واحدة من بين قصص كثيرة لنساء مثابرات وناجحات رغم المعوقات والتحديات ، خاصة في مجتمعنا الفلسطيني المليء بالتشابكات السياسية والاقتصادية والاجتماعية المعقدة .

صفاء شاهين

استمرت بالدراسة

تسارع أم فواز (48 عاما) لترى ما حل بابنيها فتتلقاها عشرات الرصاصات وترديها شهيدةً على الفور ، وما إن رأى الأخ الأوسط فوزان (46 عاما) ما حدث بدأ يصرخ بجنود القوات الخاصة المحاصرة للمنزل كى يسمحوا للإسعاف بالوصول فتكون الإجابة أن ينال هو الآخر بضع رصاصات يسقط جريحا على أثرها.

ينتهى مشهد الوابل الأحمر من الرصاص فى عتمة سماء المنزل بسقوط منجد (أبو فواز 54 عاما) ، وابنته روند (19 عاما) متأثرين ببعض الشظايا.

وكانت هى هناك ... بطلة الحدث وراويته والشاهدة على تفاصيله، كانت هيفاء هناك تعيش الواقع بكل حيثياته، تصرخ وتبكى، خوفا وحزنا وذعرا فى ذلك اليوم الذى هو أحد أيام دراستها فى الثانوية العامة.

منذ نعومة أظفارها وهى تحلم بإكمال تعليمها وتكوين شخصيتها المستقلة عن الآخرين ، ولكنها انقطعت عن الدراسة فى سن مبكرة (لم تتجاوز الرابعة عشرة) نزولا عند رغبة والديها وجدها لكى تتزوج من شاب يكبرها بأعوام قليلة. لكن زواجها لم يدم فترة طويلة لظروف سيئة كثيرة أحاطت بحياتها الزوجية أقلها أنها كانت صغيرة على مثل هذه المسؤولية ، وعادت مرة أخرى إلى حيث تقتسم مع والدتها

ترجع بنا الأيام إلى الوراء لنقف هنالك على أعتاب منزل منجد الحلبى فجر يوم 45 كانون الثانى/ يناير 2004 .

ذهبنا هناك لنشاهد عيانا آثار مجزرة حدثت وانتهت خلال لحظات كانت أسرة الحلبى فيها لم تستوعب بعد ما حدث.

كأنه كابوس ثقيل اكتملت مشاهده حين أفاق كل منهم مذعورا ينظر إلى أقرب الناس إليه يتساقطون واحدا تلو الآخر ما بين شهيد وجريح كما لو كانت ساحة معركة لا تبقى ولا تذر.

فهذا الشهيد الأول يوسف (24 عاما) ما إن يقف بمواجهة أسلحة الليزر حتى يتخطفه رصاصها فيرديه على الفور ليلحق به أخوه فواز (30 عاما) محاولا الدفاع عن أخيه فتخترق جسده أكثر من عشر رصاصات توقعه جريحا ينزف.

She went on studying

My memory goes back many days to standing next to the steps of Manjed al-Halabi's house at dawn on the day of 25th January 2006.

We went to the house right after the massacre that took place and ended within seconds even before the Halabi family understood what was going on around them.

It was like a horrific nightmare with people waking to discover what had happened, finding each other dead or wounded.

It was like a battlefield that did not leave anybody alive.

The first martyr was Yousef, aged 24. He had been standing in front of a laser weapon until its bullets seized him. It killed him immediately.

His brother, Fawwaz, aged 30, was martyred next, as he tried to defend his brother. He was hit in the body by more than 10 bullets, leaving him with bleeding wounds.

His mother, aged 48, hastened to see what had happened to her sons. She was hit by tens of bullets, and was martyred instantly.

The middle brother Fawzan, aged 26, saw what happened and shouted to the Special Forces soldiers surrounding the house to allow an ambulance to come. The answer was that they shot him. He fell to the floor wounded.

The red flood from the bullets ended in the dark sky of the household, with the collapse of Manjed (Abu Fawwaz was 54 years old) and a daughter

Rawan (19 years old), who were wounded by the fragments of the bullets.

And she was there... the hero of the event, its narrator, witness of its details. Haifa was there, living the reality in every way. She screamed and she cried, fearful, sad and terrified on that day that was one of the days of her secondary education.

From her earliest youth, she dreamed of completing her education and forming a personality independent of others. But she was taken out of school early (when she hadn't yet become 14 years old) in deference to her father's wishes. He wanted to see her married to a boy slightly older than her.

However, her marriage did not last long because there were bad circumstances. She was still young and not yet ready to have such responsibility. She returned home to take a share in the endless housework with her mother.

She tried to keep an interest in things beyond the house. So she tried more than once to return to continue her studies but every time something happened to get in the way. But she kept her decision to return to education, no matter how long it took.

46

Haifa tells in a confident voice, how in the end she was able to sit the entrance exam for the Ministry of Teaching and Education. She passed and was then able to complete her towjehi (final secondary exam).

Her time was not filled with learning and studying, of course. She says, "I lost the most important person in my life, the one who used to support me – my mother." Responsibility for the house fell on her again entirely after the death of her mother because she is the oldest daughter.

children who were hurling stones at each other. This caused a fracture in his skull and Haifa's pain for her younger brother doubled. Her other brother and sister were still in hospital for treatment. She was responsible for the home, despite her secondary exams which were, all the while, waiting for her.

Haifa describes this time by saying, "I felt that this disaster was going to kill my future as a student, and that all of the doors had closed in my face." She adds "But I depended on God and in the end I succeeded." And Haifa did succeed in her towjehi exam, with a score of 75%.

She started to work in the house by day and study by night. This was hard as she did not attend school, or have any tutoring. But she was stronger than her difficult and frustrating circumstances.

Haifa continued by saying that her studies at that time were almost impossible, and she felt almost as if she should give up. The situation became more difficult during her general exams, when the youngest of her siblings, Umar, who was 11 years old, was hit in the head by a small rock as he passed by some

Haifa continues, "I am now married and there is no doubt that I will continue my university studies every day, even though I care for my home, my husband and his children from previous marriage. The road ahead is long, but this is only the beginning."

Haifa's story is just one of many stories of women persevering and succeeding despite huge difficulties and challenges in our Palestinian society which is full of political, economic and social hurdles.

Safa' Shahin

على سطح المنزل

ارتاحت أم عاطف لقرار اتخذه ابنها ناصر بعدم الذهاب الى الجامعة فى بير زيت والبقاء فى المنزل لتناول طعام الغداء مع الأسرة ولدراسة ما عليه من إمتحانات فهو فى السنة الأخيرة ويدرس الهندسة، ودائما ينظر إليه والده ويقول له متى يأتى اليوم الذى أراك فيه بثياب التخرج يا ناصر وكان حلم وأمنيه.

استأذن ناصر من أمه ليصعد الى سطح منزلهم ليدرس وبدأت الخالة أم عاطف بإعداد الوجبة المفضلة لابنها، فهو اليوم ضيفها لم تكن تعلم انه لن يتناول الطعام بعد اليوم وان هذا الضيف سيرحل بدون رجعة.

دخلت الأم الى المطبخ وصعد ناصر الى السطح لم يمضى وقت طويل قبل أن تسمع الأم ومعها الجيران صوت رصاصة اهتز لها قلبها، وصعدت الى السطح فوجدت ابنها ممد على الأرض وفى رأسه فجوة

تنزف دماً، لقد فارق الحياة برصاصة أطلقها جندى مستهتر من الخلف استقرت فى رأسه استشهد فوراً.

لم يمر ناصر هذا اليوم عن حواجز التفتيش التى تنصب للطلاب بين ابوديس ورام الله وبير زيت لإهانتهم والتنكيل بهم وصعد فقد على السطح فأخذ نصيبه من يوم الأسير الفلسطينى.

استشهد ناصر وتناثرت أوراقه على سطح منزلهم وتناثرت معها أحلام والديه وضاعت أمانيهم وبعدها مرض والده من القهر وظل حتى توفى ولحق به.

برأيكم: كم تساوى دمعة أم فقدت عزيز.

نجاح عياد.

48

On the roof

Um 'Aatif was happy to have decided to take her son, Nasser, out of Bir Zeit University on that special day and to have him remain in the house, have lunch with his family and study for his exams. He was in the final year and studying engineering. His father always looked at him and said "When will the day come when I will see you in a graduation gown Nasser?" That was his hope and his dream.

Nasser asked his mother if he could go on to the roof of the house to study. Um 'Aatif began to prepare her son's favourite meal. Her lunch-guest did not realise that he would not eat food after today or that he would be taken away never to return again.

His mother went into the kitchen and Nasser went up on to the roof. It wasn't long before his mother and the neighbours heard the sound of a bullet. The sound shook her heart. She went onto the roof and found her son sprawled on the floor, with a crack in his head from where blood was pouring. His life had ended due to a bullet that came from a young soldier behind him and that lodged in his head. He was martyred immediately.

That day, Nasser had not gone through the checkpoint that students travelling between Abu Dis and Ramallah and Bir Zeit must go through, the checkpoint of humiliation and abuse. He had just gone and sat on the roof. That was where he took his place on Palestinian Prisoner's Day.

Nasser was martyred and his papers on the roof were scattered. With them, the dreams of his parents were scattered and their hope was lost. After his death, his father fell ill under the oppression and remained ill his death, when he was reunited with his son.

In your opinion: what is the value of the tears of a mother who has lost her darling son?

Najah Ayyad

بجانب المستوطنة

خبر استشهاده كان مفاجئة ليس فقط لأهله وإنما لكل من عرف محمود لأنه كان يتحلى بالأخلاق الحسنة، كان يحب كل الناس محمود له أصحاب كثيرون وبالذات أصدقاء أجانب، قبل استشهاده كانت هناك مجموعة متضامنين أجانب من فرنسا ومن بريطانيا والنرويج والسويد يعملون معه في المخيم الصيفي، ولما عملوا بخبر استشهاده، حضروا الى هنا الى البيت ومكثوا ثلاثة أيام لمواساة عائلته وبقوا في البيت وحاولوا أن يمنعوا الجيش الإسرائيلي من هدم المنزل لكن الجيش كان أقوى منا ومنهم وأخرجوهم من المنزل وهدموه.

الم يكن هناك أى مساعدةً او شرطةً؟

لا لم يكن بالإمكان أى شخص المساعدة لقد هدموا المنزل، الإسرائيليون يستطيعون فعل ما يريدون.

العائلات والجيران ساعدوا ببناء البيت مرة أخرى، رغم أنهم يحذرون الجميع من تقديم المساعدة لأهل أى شهيد، يحذرون من البناء في نفس المنطقة ولكن ليس في المناطق البعيدة عن مكان البيت المهدوم.

ونحن اليوم ممنوعون من مغادرة القرية، ممنوعين من دخول القدس والعمل في إسرائيل والتصاريح

نحن ممنوعين كذلك من المغادرة الى الأردن.

من بيت فوريك

لقاء مع والدة شهيد قتل على أيدى الإسرائيليون- لقد بكت طوال فترة اللقاء ومعظم القصة رويت من خلال أفراد العائلة والأصدقاء.

هذة صورة الشهيد الذى قتل بتاريخ 29\4\2003 شرقى مستوطنة ألون موريه، طبعا سمعنا خبر الاستشهاد وكانت مفاجئة، بعد الاستشهاد بيومين أتى الجيش الى البلدة الساعة الواحدة والنصف او الثانية صباحا وهدموا البيت.

هل تقصدين انه كان ينوى تفجير نفسه؟

لا...لا كان مع أصدقائه بجانب المستوطنة وقد ادعى الإسرائيليون أنهم يشكلون تهديد....... بعد فترة أيام جاء الإسرائيليون وهدموا المنزل، لقد دمروا كل شىء ولم يمنحونا الفرصة لإخراج أى شىء من المنزل.

هدموا البيت بدون ذنب او جريمة ؟

الاحتلال لا يريد مبرر لعمل أى شىء ...قبل 48 ساعة من استشهاده كان في مخيم صيفى بأريحا وكان فيه لمدة عشرة أيام مع أصحابه عادوا الى البلدة وذهبوا ليتفقدوا الأشجار حيث تم أطلقوا النار عليهم وقتلوهم.
كان الشهيد محمود طالب في جامعة القدس المفتوحة بنابلس وكان سكرتير مجلس اتحاد الطلبة ومتطوع بالإغاثة الزراعية قتل اثنان من أصدقائه معه في نفس الليلة.

الشهيد كان يؤمن بقيام دولة فلسطين على حدود 67 يعنى ما كان يحمل فكر متطرف بل يحمل فكر يسارى ويؤمن بالحياة وقيام دولتين دولة إسرائيل ودولة فلسطين تعيش جنبا الى جنب على حدود 67.

في فترة الدراسة الجامعية كان سكرتير كتلة اتحاد الطلبة التابعة لحزب الشعب جامعة القدس المفتوحة قضى حياته بالعمل السياسى والجماهيرى مع الناس يعنى هو كان متطوع بالإغاثة الزراعية ومؤسسات أخرى فقضى حياته يعتبر نفسه دائما للناس.

دائما كان يقول يود أن ينهى دراسته الجامعة وانه لا يفكر بالزواج كان يود تعلم الموسيقى والسفر ولم يكن يخطر بباله انه سيكون شهيد.

الشهيد
محمود أمين غلمي

50

Near the settlement

A meeting with the mother of a young man killed by the Israelis. She cried throughout the interview and most of the story was told by family and friends.

This is a photo of the martyr. He was killed on 29th April 2003 in the east of the Alon Moreh settlement. Of course, we heard about him being killed and it was a surprise for us. Two days afterwards, the army came at 1.30 or 2am, and destroyed the house.

You mean he was going in order to blow himself up?
No no, he was with his friends, near to the settlement. The Israelis felt that they represented a danger to them. Later the Israeli army came and destroyed the house. They destroyed everything in it and did not give us a chance to take anything out of the house.

So they destroyed the house without there having been any crime?
The Occupation does not need a justification for doing anything. Forty-eight hours before he was martyred, he was on a summer camp in Jericho for 10 days, with his friends. They came back and they went round into the trees, and they were shot.

The martyr, Mahmoud, was a student of Al-Quds Open University in Nablus. He was a secretary for the Student Union Council and a volunteer in Agricultural Relief. Two of his friends were also killed on the same night.

In his life, he believed in the establishment of a Palestinian state within the borders of 1967. He didn't have extreme views but rather he had left-wing views, believing in life and establishing two states, the Israeli state and the Palestinian state, living side by side according to the borders of 1967.

He lived only one third of his life. When he was at university he was a secretary of the People's Party group in the student union at Al Quds Open University. He died doing political work concerning the people. He was a volunteer for Agricultural Relief and other foundations. He died having taken nothing for his own life and always considering himself to be for the people.

There was a time when he used to say that when he finished university he would not think of marriage but rather he would think of what he wanted to learn of music, travel and sport. He never thought of martyring himself or doing anything like that.

The news of his martyrdom was a surprise not only to his family but also to everyone that knew Mahmoud because he used to have such excellent morals and his life had never annoyed or upset anyone. In fact, everybody loved Mahmoud and he had many friends, particularly foreign friends. They heard the news and came here to the house and slept here for three days. That was a difficult time and they gave us and his family sympathy.

They were in the house when the Israeli army arrived. They tried to stop them destroying the house but the army was stronger than us and them and it sent them away. Many people were incredibly upset.

Was there no police, no enquiry, nothing?
No, no, it is finished. They can do what they like. The families, neighbours and some organisations helped to build a new house. This is despite the fact that the Israeli military warned anyone against providing help to the family of any martyr. That is how people do things here, they help each other.

If this happens, the Israelis stop people building where they have destroyed a house. And they will never let any one in the family go out of this area. Not to work in Israel, not to Jerusalem, not to Jordan. Leaving is forbidden... we can never go.

From Beit Fourik

في المسجد

كاميراتهم من قبل الشرطة الإسرائيلية يريد الفلسطينيون أن يخبروا كل العالم عن الأوضاع المزرية التى يعيشونها ليس فقط فى القدس ولكن فى كل فلسطين المحتلة.

سماح شقيرات

أود أن أتكلم عن الوضع الحالى للمسجد الأقصى والذى يعد من أقدس المقدسات لدى الفلسطينيين، معظم الفلسطينيون اليوم ممنوعين من الصلاة فيه تحديدا الفلسطينيون الذين يحملون الهوية الخضراء والذين لا يستطيعون الوصول الى مدينة القدس بدون تصريح.

فى الوقت الذى يسمح فيه لليهود من الوصول الى أى مكان يريدون وتحديدا هذا المسجد والذى هو هدف للمصادرة والتدمير لبناء ما يدعون انه هيكلهم المزعوم ولهذا يحاول الجنود الإسرائيليون اقتحام المسجد فى كل عام مما يؤدى الى حدوث مواجهات مع المصلين داخل ساحات المسجد.

فمن جهة يحاول المصلين حماية المسجد بكل ما تصل إليه أيديهم من حجارة وأخشاب وحتى الأحذية ومن الجانب الآخر يستخدم الجنود الإسرائيليون الأسلحة النارية تجاههم ويعتقلون الشبان ويعتدون على الصحافيين.

فى الشهر الماضى تكررت المواجهات مرة أخرى وكانت الإصابات فى الجانب الفلسطينى وكل العالم شاهد هذة الأحداث ولم يحرك ساكن أكثر من تسعة وأربعون مصلى أصيبوا وخمس صحافيين تم الاعتداء عليهم وكسرت

فى المسجد

سيدة بريطانية تصف حادثة سمعت عنها وأثرت فيها خلال زيارة النساء الى فلسطين مع مشروع قصص من أمهاتنا .

أصيبت سوسن وأمها بأقدامهن أثناء أدائهما للصلاة فى المسجد الأقصى، بعد أن أطلق جنود إسرائيليون النار عليهن.

لازالت آثار الإصابة بادية على قدم سوسن، تعانى أم سوسن من ارتفاع بضغط الدم ومن الإصابة التى حدثت فى المسجد، سوسن قلقة جدا على أمها.

روز

In the Mosque

I would like to talk about the recent situation in Al Aqsa Mosque, which is the holiest place in Palestine. Nevertheless, most Palestinians are forbidden from practising their religious right, specially Palestinians from the West Bank, who can't reach it without a travel permit.

On the other hand, the Jewish extremists are allowed to enter it whenever they wish, as they want to capture this place and destroy it, to build a structure which is a temple instead of a mosque.

That's why they enter the parks of the Aqsa mosque every year, to provoke the Muslims praying there, under the protection of the Israeli soldiers and police. This causes the people who are praying to face them, using stones, wood and even shoes. On the other hand, the Israeli soldiers shoot at them, hit the journalists and even take young men to prison.

Last month, the same story was repeated again and the injuries were only on the side of the weaponless Palestinians, while the whole world watched these events without moving or caring. Over forty-nine people were injured and five journalists were beaten in one morning, and had their cameras broken by the police.

I met Sawsun when I visited Palestine with the Stories from our Mothers project

Sawsun and her mother were both shot in the leg when they were praying in the Al Aqsa Mosque. This was after Israeli soldiers opened fire in the Mosque.

Sawsun still has a bullet wound in her leg. Her mother is ill and suffers from hypertension and a similar wound. Sawsun cares for her.

Ros

55

The Palestinian nation wants to tell everyone in the world about this situation, to show the conditions they are suffering from, not only in Jerusalem but all through Palestine.

ولادتي والجرو الذي عاش معنا

في يوماً ماطر بارد من شهر كانون ثاني، ولدت في بيتي في مخيم الدهيشة.

كانت الولادة صعبة جداً طويلة ومؤلمة جداً لأمي، جدتي حضرت للمساعدة، اعتقدت أمي كما قالت لي أنني ببشرة بيضاء وشعر أشقر، لم تفهم أمي لماذا تغير لون بشرتي وشعري بهذا الشكل.

بعد عشرة أيام من ولادتي، حاصر الجنود الإسرائيليون بيتنا، بدأ كلبنا بالنباح بشكل هستيري ومستمر، تساءلت أمي عن سبب نباح الكلب بهذا الشكل الهستيري حيث أنه أيضا أزعج طفلتيها التي بدأت بالبكاء، مما وتر والدتي، حملتني أمي وخرجت خارج البيت فوجدت الجنود الإسرائيليون وقد حاصروا البيت، طبعاً أذعرها المنظر، وهي لا زالت تحملني، وحاولت تهدئة الكلب، سألت الجنود عن سبب وجودهم وما يريدون.

طلب الجنود من أمي أن تحزم ما تستطيع من أغراض المنزل

لأن هناك أمر بالهدم لمنزلنا، أدهش طلبهم أمي التي قالت: (لا يمكنكم فعل ذلك، زوجي ليس في المنزل، ولدى أحد عشر ابن في المدرسة).

قام احد الجنود بضرب الكلب بكعب بندقيته مما أخرج عينا الكلب، وقد أثار هذا الفعل غضب أمي التي لم تستطع فعل شيء. قامت بوضعي مع قريبتها التي كانت موجودة والتي حاولت منعي من البكاء، بمساعدة الجيران أخرجت أمي ما استطاعت من أغراض بيتنا ووضعتها عند جيراننا ليحتفظوا بها كأمانه.

رحلت أمي من بيتنا الذي حصلنا عليه من وكالة الغوث ودمره الإسرائيليون، أحد أشقائي كان معتقل لدى الإسرائيليين لأنه كان ينتمي للجبهة الشعبية لتحرير فلسطين، حيث تعتبر هذة تهمة وجريمة بقوانين الإسرائيليين، حكم عليه بالسجن لمدة خمس عشرة سنة ولكن تم إطلاق سراحه بعد سبعة سنوات كان عمرة خمس عشرة عام عندما أعتقل.

استضافتنا ابنة عمي وزوجها في بيتهم لمدة قصيرة، لكن ذلك كان صعب عليهم لأننا عائلة كبيرة، وكان الوضع صعبا علينا لم نشعر بالراحة على اعتبار أننا شاركناهم في بيتهم المكون من غرفتين. لقد كان علينا أن نعيش بهذا الوضع لمدة أربع عشرة سنة.

صباح إخميس

56

My birth and Bobby who was raised with me

I was born in January at home in Deheishah camp.

On a very rainy cold January day my grandmother came to help, and my birth was difficult, long and painful. My mother thought I was very white, I even had blond hair, and now she cannot understand why I have changed so much.

Ten days later, Israeli soldiers came and Bobby the dog started to bark loudly and continued. So my mother wondered what was happening. This made me cry and my mother was even more distressed, so she picked me up and went outside. She found that our house was surrounded by Israeli soldiers. Obviously she was terrified. While holding on to me, and trying to calm Bobby, the dog, she asked them what they wanted.

They demanded that she should pack up all the essential items and move out because they had orders to demolish our house. She was frantic and said, "You can't do that – My husband isn't here. I have eleven children and they are at school."

One soldier hit Bobby maliciously with the end of his rifle and his eye came out. My mother was even more distressed and didn't know what to do. She managed to give me to my cousin who tried to stop my crying. Together with the neighbours, she then took everything she could manage from home and put it with the neighbours for safe-keeping.

She then had to go and our UNWRA home was demolished. One of my brothers was in prison because he was a member of PFLP and this is considered a crime by the Israelis. His sentence was fifteen years but he was released after seven years. He was fifteen years old when he was arrested.

My cousin and her husband accommodated us for a short period but it was very difficult for them as we were such a big family. And very difficult for us as we felt very uncomfortable, forcing them to share their two rooms. We had to stay living in these conditions for fourteen years.

Sabah Ikhmayees

Left: Old City, Hebron

على اليسار: البلدة القديمة. الخليل

57

جارنا

لكن المعلومات التي بحوزتهم كانت دقيقةً وبدأت معركةٌ بينهم وبين هذا الشاب حيث استطاع أن يقتل عدد من جنودهم، داهم الجنود بيتنا مرةً أخرى واخذوا زوجي وأطفالي ووضعوهم بينهم وبين بيت الشاب حيث كان الرصاص يأتي من كل اتجاه وظل هذا الشاب يقاوم من الساعة الثالثة وحتى التاسعة صباحاً حتى استشهد.

على الرغم من مقتله فقد اعتقل الجيش الإسرائيلي زوجته وزوجي وشاب آخر كان متواجد معه ولم يكتفوا بذلك بل بدأوا يفجرون أبواب المنازل وهدموا بعضها حتى وصلوا الى منزل الشاب وهدموه.

في اليوم التالي وعندما حضرت والدة الشاب الى بقايا منزله قالت انه ترك بيته الجميل في كفر راعي وجاء للعيش في هذا البيت الصغير من اجل فلسطين التي طالما ضحى الشباب بأرواحهم فداها هذة هي حكاية جارنا إياد صوالحة الذي سكن بجانبنا ولم نعرفه.

سهى ناصر كميل

أريد أن أروي لكم قصة شخص عاش لمدة أربعة أشهر في جوارنا كان بجانب بيتنا منزل فارغ قال لنا أصحابة أن مستأجر جديد سوف يسكن فيه مع عروسه وفعلا هذا ما حدث، دخل شاب ومعه فتاه وسكنا في المنزل.

وبعد عدة أيام بدأ الجيش الإسرائيلي بمحاصرة مدينة جنين والبحث عن شاب يدعى إياد صوالحة من كفر راعي قضاء جنين.

وصل الحصار الى حارتنا وهي منطقة قديمةٍ في مدينة جنين واستمر الحصار لمدة سبعة عشر يوماً ودخل شهر رمضان ونحن محاصرين.

في إحدى الليالي استيقظت في الصباح الباكر لأحضر طعام السحور وإذا بالجيش الإسرائيلي وكلابهم يحاصرون المكان وما أن أشعلت النور حتى سمعت صوت انفجار قوي قبل أن يدخل الجيش بيتنا ومعهم صورة لشاب يسألون عنه وبالرغم من انه جارنا إلا أننا قلنا أننا لا نعرفه.

58

Our neighbour

I want to tell a story about a neighbour who lived next to us for four months.

There was an empty house next to our house, and this man came and rented it with his bride.

A few days after he rented that house, the Jews came and they surrounded the city (Jenin), looking for a man called Eyad Sawalha from Kufr Ra'eh, a village near Jenin. They started to go from one neighbourhood to another until they reached our neighbourhood. When they arrived at our neighbourhood, an old part of Jenin city, the siege they imposed remained for seventeen days, and during this time the month of Ramadan started.

One night I woke up to prepare suhour (the breakfast before the fast). When I looked out of the window, I saw the Israeli soldiers and their dogs all over the place around us. I turned on the light, and I heard a huge explosion.

The soldiers entered our house. One of them had a photo of a young man, and he asked me about him. Although he was my neighbour, I said that I didn't know him.

Suddenly there was gun shooting around us, and a battle between these soldiers and that young man. The young man managed to kill many of the soldiers.

The soldiers entered my house and they took my husband and my children and they put them between the two houses. There was still gun-shooting from two directions. That young man continued resisting from three in the morning till nine in the morning, when he was killed. Although they killed him, they took his wife and they took my husband and another man.

When his family knew about what happened with their son, they came to what remained of his house and his mother said "He left his beautiful house in our village, and he came to live in this crowded, tiny house because he wanted to hide and to continue his fight against the occupation."

This is the story of our neighbour, whom we did not manage to know.

Suha Nasser Kmeil

ابني

عندما وصلنا الى المخيم كنا نعيش جميعاً فى غرفة واحدة، ثلاث عشر شخص فى غرفة واحدة

لا زالت احلم فى العودة الى أرضنا. لقد ذهبت الى بلدتنا جاندو وقد رأيت الإسرائيليون يستمتعون بأرضنا التى سرقوها منا. لقد حولوا جزء منها الى متنزه. بدأ أولادى باللعب فى الحقل المجاور لكن الإسرائيليون أمرونا بالمغادرة حتى وهى أرضنا.

بمشيئة الله ستعود أرضنا وكل أراضى فلسطين الى أصحابها. لازالوا يسرقون الأراضى فى القدس والمسجد الأقصى منا. هذا المسجد هو رمز عزتنا ومصدر قوتنا للبقاء.

لقد عانيت من كل هذا ... لقد أصابوا ابنى فى عينه وقد فقد البصر فيها أود أن سأروى لكم كيف أصيب ابنى من قبل الاحتلال وما حصل معى.

قبل سنة وثلاثة أشهر اقتحم الجيش الإسرائيلى غزة دمروها وقتلوا أهلها وفى ذلك الحين كنا فى زيارة لأهل زوجى فى القدس ....وعندما رجعنا الى المخيم أوقف الجيش الإسرائيلى الحافلات عند الحاجز وسرنا على الأقدام.

كانت تجرى فى المخيم مظاهرة ضد تدمير غزة وبدأ الجيش الإسرائيلى بإطلاق قنابل الغاز والرصاص المطاطى تجاه المتظاهرين وابنى يقول أسرعى يا أمى اختنقنا من الغاز.

رأيت ابنى وهو يسقط على الأرض وتسيل دماؤه من عينه وفقد الوعى.

نقل الى مستشفى العيون فى غرفة العمليات وكان عنده نزيف حاد بالشبكية ومكث فى المستشفى لمدة عشر أيام والآن لا يرى بعينه.

أتمنى من الله أن يكون لها علاج وإذا لزم الأمر أن أفقد عينى وتوضع مكان عينه الذى فقدها حتى أراه سعيدا فى حياته لان قلبى يحترق عليه وأخاف أن يفقد عينه الأخرى من أى شىء.

إعتماد وهبة

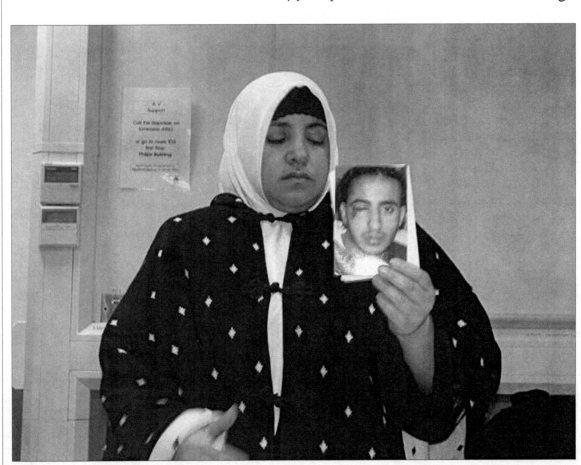

My son

When we moved into the refugee camp, we were all in one room – thirteen people in one room.

I still dream now of returning to my land. Two months ago, I went to our village, Jandu, and I saw Israelis there enjoying the lands which they stole from us. They have made some of it into parks. My children started playing in the fields but they told them to leave, even though it is our land.

God willing our land, and all of Palestine, will return to us. They are still stealing Jerusalem and the Al-Aqsa Mosque away from us. That mosque is a symbol of our greatness and our staying power.

I suffer from all of this. They injured my son in his eye and he lost it and so now he cannot see with it. I want to tell you how my son was injured during the Occupation.

It happened one year and three months ago when the Israeli army invaded Gaza, destroying it and killing its people. At that time, we visited my husband's family in Jerusalem. When we came back to the refugee camp, the Israeli army stopped the cars at the checkpoint and we had to go on foot.

There was a demonstration against the attack on Gaza City and the Israeli army started throwing gas bombs and shooting at the demonstrators. My son said, "Faster mum, hurry up," but we couldn't tolerate the gas.

Then I saw my son falling to the floor and blood was coming out of his eyes. He was unconscious.

He was taken to the ophthalmic hospital in Jerusalem to the operation room. He had a haemorrhage in the retina of his eye and stayed in the hospital for 10 days. Now he can't see with his eye.

I pray to God that he will be cured. I would have my eye removed so that it could be given to my son who has lost his eye so that I can see him happy in his life. My heart is burning for him and I am very worried that he will lose his other eye.

E'temad Wahbeh

عنف المستوطنين

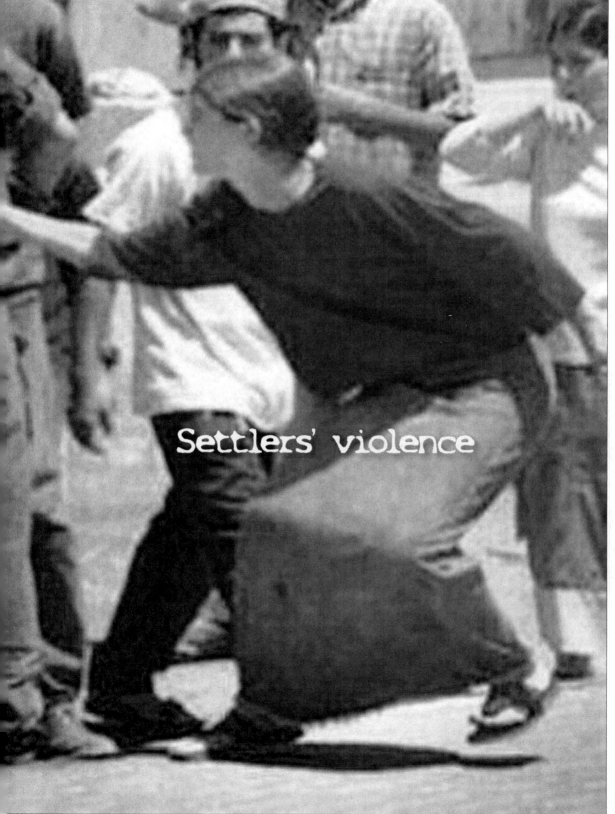

Settlers' violence

قوتها ومقاومةً من يريدون أخذ أرضها. بعد ذلك استخدم المستوطنين القوة وقاموا بالاعتداء عليها وضربها قبل أن يغادروا ومعهم الحمار.

هذة الهجمات الوحشية تعتبر مألوفة جداً للفلسطينيين وتحدث فى كل مكان فى أماكن تواجد المستوطنات، وما يختلف هنا هو انه عنف منظم وبإشراف الدولة، فلا يوجد شرطة حيث من الممكن طلب المساعدة منهم، لا يوجد عدالة.

زرنا فى هذة البلدة أيضا سيدةً لديها عشرةَ أبناء، زوجها نجار. قررت السلطات الإسرائيلية بأن نصف بيتهم ليس قانونيا، جاء الجيش الإسرائيلى عدة مرات ودمروا ورشته

وعمله، فى العام الماضى قررت السلطات الإسرائيلية بأن هناك سبعةً وأربعون بيت فى البلدة غير قانونية، بمعنى أن سكان هذة البيت سيتم إخلاءهم وسيتم هدم المنازل فى أى وقت.

لقد كان مذهلاً مدى إصرار الناس على الحياة بكرامة، ومدى إيمانهم بحقوقهم الآدمية وتضامننا معهم فى هذة الظروف القاهرة. فى كل يوم يزيد انهيارنا بقوة وإصرار الشعب الفلسطينى مع وجود كل هذا التهديد المباشر لحياتهم، فى كل يوم علمنا الفلسطينيون معنى أن نكون آدميين.

كارين ريتير [بريطانيا]

في القرى

فى هذا الجزء من العالم لا يمكن الجمع بين الجنة والجحيم فى مكان واحد.

لقد تم إخبارنا بأنه حتى فى هذا اليوم حضرت سيارة عسكرية الى التلة المجاورة لتقوم بأعمال مراقبة، بعد ذلك أخبرتنا مضيفتنا بان إحدى بنات أخوتها ولدت حين رفض الجنود الإسرائيليون السماح لوالديها المرور الى المستشفى فى طولكرم، لحسن الحظ فإن الطفلة وأمها تمكنا من المرور بهذه التجربة بسلام، لكن كان هناك العديد من الحالات التى كانت نتائجها ميتة.

فى المساء شرح لنا مضيفنا عن ذلك الشىء المستطيل الموضوع على الأرض فى غرفة الجلوس، لم تكن قطعة الزينة هذة إلا صاروخ إسرائيلى تم إطلاقه من قبل الجيش الإسرائيلى واخترق جدار منزل العائلة مما احدث فتحة كبيرة فى الجدار قبل عدة سنوات، لقد احدث انفجار هذا الصاروخ دمار وهلع كبير عند أفراد الأسرة، إلا أنهم قرروا بعد ذلك تجميع أجزاء هذا الصاروخ ووضعوه فى البيت تعبيرا عن هذة الذكرى الأليمة.

فى اليوم التالى زرنا بلدة الساوية، كان الاستقبال الذى حظينا به مميزا جدا، تجمع بعض أهالى البلدة فى مبنى البلدة وألقى رئيس البلدة كلمة ترحيب بنا، فيما قدمت لنا هدايا من التطريز الفلسطينى من جمعية نساء البلدة.

بعد وجبة رائعة من الطعام، أقيمت على شرفنا رقصات من الدبكة الشعبية الفلسطينية، قبل أن نتوجه الى بيت مضيفنا لتلك الليلة..... لقد كانت الضيافة رائعة وتبادل الحديث مع فنجان الشاى والقهوة.

أخبرنا والد مضيفنا بان العائلة كانت تمتلك مساحة واسعة من الأراضى والتى يمكن رؤيتها من بعيد، ولا يمكن الوصول إليها بسبب بناء المستوطنات الإسرائيلية غير الشرعية عليها. لقد أخبرنا بان بلدة الساوية خسرت حوالى 75% من أراضيها لصالح المستوطنات الإسرائيلية والتى احتلت سفوح التلال الممتدة حول البلدة.

أخبرتنا أم صديقنا ما حدث لها قبل سنوات حين كانت فى أرضها المزروعة بأشجار الزيتون، قدم المستوطنون إليها وطلبوا منها أن تعطيهم حمارها وأن تغادر الأرض، لكنها ومن منطلق كونها موجودة فى أرضها وبين أشجارها وان هذا الحمار ملك لها فقد قررت تجميع

فى اليوم الخامس من زيارتنا توجهنا الى الشمال، لقد تفرقنا الى مجموعتين، واحدة ذهبت الى عزون والثانية الى بيت ليد، كنت أنا فى المجموعة الثانية، بعد أن زرنا مراكز فى أبو ديس والقدس ورام الله وبيت لحم والخليل نحن الآن ذاهبون فى اتجاه آخر.

بدت بيت ليد وديعة وهادئة لا ضجيج ولا تلوث، بدا أن الزمان قد توقف هنا، كانت هناك صور تأخذك الى الماضى الى العهد البابلى، سيدتان يرتدين الثوب القديم ورجل عجوز يعتمر كوفية يجلس فى الظل خارج منزله، رجل آخر يركب حمارا يقود أغنامه الى أسفل الطريق، للحظة شعرت أنى فى إجازة.

عند وصولنا كان فى استقبالنا رئيس المجلس البلدى وعدد من رجال البلدة بنا، حيث ألقى رئيس المجلس كلمة ترحيب، بعدها قاموا بعرض محاضرة احتوت على حقائق وأرقام عن بلدة بيت ليد. خلال احتسائنا للقهوة مع مستضيفينا علمنا انه كانت هناك بلدة أخرى تدعى خربة بيت ليد بجانب البحر، أنشئت من قبل بعض سكان البلدة الحالية وقد تم تدميرها خلال النكبة فى العام 1948. فى النهاية فنحن فى فلسطين وهناك المزيد من القصص عن مصادرة الأراضى وتهجير اللاجئين.

بعد هذا الحديث توجهنا الى البيت الذى يستضيفنا على وجبة الطعام، مرة أخرى عاد انطباع كوننا فى أجازة يساورنى، الهواء النقى وجمال الطبيعة، فى الطريق أطربت مسامعنا الأهازيج الريفية لعائلة كانت تعمل فى الحديقة الخارجية للمنزل.

حضرت وصفية عثمان أشهى المأكولات لنا حيث طبخت مسخن وهى عبارة عن طبق كبير شبيه بالبيتسا مع دجاج ونواه الصنوبر وبهارات السماك المصنوع فى منطقة طولكرم.

تعمل وصفية ومجموعة من نساء البلدة على الحفاظ على التقاليد والتراث فى البلدة من خلال إنتاج الأشغال اليدوية وأكيد الطبخ جزء من ها التراث. فى ساعات ما بعد الظهر شاركنا فى ورشة عمل فى مركز نسوى فى البلدة حيث علمتنا ريما كيف نعمل الورود من الأسلاك والخرز. وهنا تمكنا من الحصول على هدية جميلة ملفوف بورق زهرى وهى عبارة عن صابون مصنوع محليا من زيت الزيتون.

كم كانت هذة البلدة جميلة وأهلها مضيافين، وكم من الممكن أن تكون هذة البلدة مسالمة ولكن سرعان ما تذكرنا انه حتى

In the villages

On the fifth day we set off for a tour north. We split into two groups, one went to Azzoun, the other to Beit Leed. I was in the latter group. After having seen the urban centres Abu Dis, Jerusalem, Ramallah, Bethlehem and Hebron we now ventured out to a rural destination.

Beit Leed seemed tranquil and peaceful, no noise or air pollution, time seemed to have stood still here. There were images which take you back to biblical times, a couple of women in traditional dresses, an old man with a keffiyeh sitting in the shade outside his house, a man on a donkey driving a herd of sheep down the road. For a moment it felt like a real holiday.

We were welcomed by the mayor and a few other men in suits who gave us a talk and slide show about the history and lots of statistical facts about Beit Leed. While we were sipping coffee we learnt that there used to be another village with the same name Khirbat Beit Leed by the sea, founded by people from this Beit Leed and destroyed during the Nakba May 1948. We were in Palestine after all and heard more stories of loss of land and property and refugees.

After this talk we walked down the road to the house where we were expected for lunch. Again this temporary feeling of holiday, the clean air, the beauty of the landscape. We passed a house where we heard the voices of a family out in their garden, it was almost idyllic.

Wasfiya Othman had prepared a most amazing culinary treat for us: mussakhan, a large pizza-like dish with pine kernels and the spice zumac, which is a speciality of the Tulkarem area.

Wasfiya and the women of the village are very active in keeping traditional crafts alive and cookery is part of this. In the afternoon we took part in a workshop at the local women's centre where Remah taught us to make flowers out of wire and beads. Here we also had the opportunity to buy hand made olive oil soap beautifully presented with pink ribbon.

How beautiful this country and the people are! And how peaceful it could be! But soon enough we were reminded that even here heaven and hell are never far apart.

We were told that earlier that day an Israeli army vehicle had been patrolling the hill opposite. Later we learnt that one of the children, a niece of our host, had been born at a checkpoint when the soldiers refused the parents passage to the clinic in Tulkarem. Fortunately mother and child survived this trauma, but there are reports of other cases which resulted in fatalities.

In the evening our hosts explained an oblong object which was standing on the floor next to a tall vase in the beautiful living room. This 'ornament' was a rocket which was fired by the Israeli army a few years ago and had smashed through the wall leaving a gaping hole in the corner of the house. It had exploded causing much fear and distress to the family who later had it reassembled and glued together as a reminder of this terrible incident.

The next day we visited As Sawiya. The reception we received in the village was overwhelming. Villagers had assembled in the municipal building where the mayor gave a welcome speech and we were presented with embroidery from the local women›s association.

After a wonderful feast of a meal we were treated to a display of dabkeh dance before we were taken to our hosts' home. It was lovely to retire here and talk over refreshing sage tea and coffee.

Our friend's father told us that the family used to own the land they can now only view from the distance but not enter because of the illegal settlements. We were told that As Sawiya has lost 75% of its land to the settlements which occupy all the hills around.

Our friend's mother then told us what happened to her a few years ago when she was in her olive

grove. Settlers came and demanded that she gave them her donkey and told her to leave. Strong as she is and in the knowledge that she was on her land attending to her trees she stood her ground and defended her land and her donkey. The settlers then used violence and knocked her down and beat her up and went off with the donkey.

Violent attacks like this are not unique to Palestine and can happen everywhere; what is different here is that this is state-endorsed violence, there is no police which Palestinians can expect help from, there is no justice.

We also visited the house of a woman in the same village who has ten children. Her husband is a carpenter. The Israelis regard one half of this house as 'illegal' and the army has turned up on several occasions destroying all his work. Last year forty-seven households in the village were issued with "illegal" notices, meaning that the inhabitants can be evicted and the houses demolished at any time.

It is amazing how people can maintain so much dignity and beauty and so much faith in our common humanity under these terrible conditions. Every day we are amazed at the strength and the dignity Palestinians maintain in the face of the constant threats to their lives. Every day Palestinians have taught us what humanity means.

Karin Reiter [UK]

ذاهب الى الدكان

أنا من البلدة القديمة فى الخليل وأسكن فيها من تسع سنوات، معاناتنا فى البلدة القديمة كبيرة جداً فهى محاطة بالمستوطنين من كل الجهات مع تواجد الجيش الإسرائيلى على مدار الساعة فيها.

فى البلدة القديمة أطفالنا يعانون فلا يوجد لهم مجال للعب او الخروج من البلدة القديمة. اغلب الأوقات منطقة البلدة القديمة تكون تحت منع التجول او منطقة عسكرية مغلقة بالليل، قبل يومين أغلقوا منطقة البلدة القديمة لمدة ثلاث ساعات.

نحن سكان البلدة القديمة لا نعرف سبب الإغلاق وانتشار الجيش حول بيوتنا ولكن نحن متأكدون بان الهدف هو ترهيب وتخويف الناس خاصة الاطفال والأمهات.

طبعاً البلدة القديمة كانت لأهل الخليل حتى اقتحمها الجيش الإسرائيلى وقسمها كما تم تقسيم الحرم الإبراهيمى الشريف بعد المجزرة التى ارتكبها متطرف إسرائيلى بحق المصلين المسلمين فيه فى العام 1994.

فى يوم جمعة وأثناء شهر رمضان دخل الصهيونى المتطرف باروخ غولدشتاين وبدأ بإطلاق النار على الناس وهم يصلون حيث قتل العشرات من المصلين داخل الحرم الإبراهيمى وأصيب العشرات لا يزال العديد منهم يعانون إعاقات من اثر الرصاص.

بعد هذه الحادثة قررت السلطات الإسرائيلية تقسيم الحرم الإبراهيمى حيث وضعوا حواجز على بوابات الحرم وجعلوا المسلمين غرفة واحدة للصلاة واعتبروا الأجزاء المتبقية أماكن لصلاة المتطرفين اليهود والمستوطنين لتبدأ بعد ذلك حملة استيطان محمومة ويدخل المئات من المستوطنين اليهود الى داخل البلدة القديمة من الخليل.

كنتيجة طبيعية لها الاستهداف وما خلقه من مشاكل للمواطنين الفلسطينيين هناك بدأ الآلاف من سكان البلدة القديمة بالرحيل خوفاً منها من قمع الجيش الإسرائيلى وتسلط المستوطنين.

معاناة سكان البلدة القديمة اربع وعشرون ساعة وفى كل يوم، الجيش متواجد يأتون فى الليل الى منازلنا يقتحمون الأبواب، اذا استعصت الأبواب يقتحمون المنازل عن طرق السقف على اعتبار أن بيوتنا ملتصقة ببعضها وملاصقة لأسوار البلدة القديمة، لا يراعون وجود أطفال نيام او خصوصية الناس فى بيوتهم.

يخرجون الرجال ويجبروهم على خلع ملابسهم والوقوف فى البرد القارص وأيديهم مرفوعة وفى أحيان كثيرة يتعرضوا للضرب. من اخطر الأمور التى تواجهها المرأة الفلسطينية فى البلدة القديمة فى الخليل هو كيفية حماية أطفالها فى ظل وجود المستوطنين بحماية الجيش.

اما عن تجاربى الشخصية فى البلدة القديمة أننى أرسلت ابنى الى الدكان أثناء منع التجول الذى فرضه الجيش الإسرائيلى ليشترى حليب لشقيقه الصغير وكان ذلك فى أحد أعياد اليهود، فى طريقة الى الدكان مر ابنى الذى كان يبلغ الخامسة من العمر بعدد من المستوطنين اليهود وهم طبعاً بحراسة كاملة من الجيش الإسرائيلى فطلبوا منه أن يعود الى البيت لوجود منع تجول. لم يفهم ابنى معنى منع التجول وقرر متابعة المسير الى الدكان فما كان من الضابط الإسرائيلى المسئول إلا أن ضربه وطرحه بالأرض.

حاولت جارتى التى تسكن مقابل الشارع أن تساعد طفلى وأخبرتنى بان الجيش احتجزوا ابنى فلم اصدق إلا بعد ان خرجت الى الشارع ورايتهم يضربوه صرخت بهم لماذا تضربوه فقال الجندى (انه منع تجول وهو يسرى على الصغار والكبار).

سارة الطرشان

Going to the shop

I am from the old city of Hebron and I have lived there for nine years. In the old city, we suffer a lot as the settlers surround it on all sides and the army is there twenty-four hours a day. We also suffer because of our children. Our children do not have space to play in or escape in the old city.

Most of the time, it is forbidden to move around the old city or it becomes a closed area. Two days ago they closed the old city for three hours, making it a closed military zone. We do not know why they do this – it is only to intimidate the people, the children and the mothers of the old city.

Of course, the old city was, originally, for the people of Hebron itself. But the army came and divided up the Ibrahimi Mosque after the massacre in 1994. The massacre was on a Friday when Muslims were praying; it was Ramadan. A settler called Baruch Goldstein came to the mosque and began to fire bullets at the people as they prayed; there were dozens of martyrs. There are also still people now who are disabled because they were shot.

After that incident, the Ibrahimi Mosque was divided and the army put up checkpoints . They left only one room for Muslims to pray in and the rest of the Mosque was taken to be a synagogue. Now we always see settlers coming in to consolidate their presence in the old city. They want to cause problems until the Palestinians feel they have to leave the old city.

Every family in the old city, mine included, suffers under the military presence twenty-four hours a day. Even in the night, as

we are sleeping, they break down our front door. The roofs of the houses in the old city are joined together and linked to the city wall – you can go from one to the other. If the doors are not opened, then the soldiers enter from the roof and they come in, even if your children are sleeping. They always come at 2 or 3 in the middle of the night.

They take our men and our husbands; they take off their clothes and make them stand in the cold, raising their hands and with their legs against the wall. Sometimes they beat them and sometimes they say to us that we must wake our children if they are sleeping.

Now, one of the most dangerous things that a woman suffers from in the old city is how to deal with her children in the face of the settlers and the army that protect them.

Four years ago my son was going to the shop at a time when there was a curfew. He wanted to bring milk for his younger brother. It was the day of the Jewish Sabbath when the settlers are everywhere in the old city with the protection of the military.

My son was very young. The Jews said to him "Go back"; but he didn't know the meaning of a curfew. so he didn't answer them and walked between the settlers and the area that I was in as he wanted to go to the shop. An Israeli officer came and hit my son. He was only 5 years old and in the kindergarten.

He hit him and threw him on the ground. Our neighbour, Um Khaldun, whose house is on the street, came and told me that the soldiers had hit my son; I just couldn't believe her because he was so young.

I went out and saw what was going on. I said "Why did you do that, he's a little boy?" The soldier said "The curfew is for everybody; the young and the old, you can't go out."

Sarah Al-Tarshan

ربط بشجرة

بيت فوريك تعاني من الاحتلال منذ البداية وهناك الكثير من القصص عن بلدة بيت فوريك ... عدد سكانها 12 ألف نسمة وتحيطها ثلاث مستوطنات اتمار ، ألون موريه، ومخورة، وحاجز إسرائيلي بالوسط بين بيت فوريك ونابلس.

وهناك الكثير من القصص حصلت على هذا الحاجز مع أهالي بيت فوريك وهناك الكثير من السيدات أنجبن على الحاجز وحصل نزيف لبعض السيدات وتوفيت امرأتان على الحاجز وتوفيت ابنة أختي بين أيدي وعمرها 6 سنوات وكانت مريضة بالزائدة حيث منع الجيش الإسرائيلي سيارة الإسعاف من الوصول إليها وتوفيت معنا داخل السيارة.

هناك قصة عن الزيتون والأراضي محمد زلموط خطاطبة ذهب الى أرضه ليجمع الزيتون وقدم بعض المستوطنين إليه قتلوه وربطوه بالشجرة ووضعوه على الأرض وغطوا جسده بالحجارة لم يعرف مصيره حتى اليوم التالي.

قصة أخرى حصلت هناك في قرية صغيرة قرب بيت فوريك من مدة شهرين أبطالها خمس وثلاثين بدويه قدم الجيش الإسرائيلي ودمر كل الخيام وسرق الأغنام ودمر كل شيء.

أخرجوهم من بيوتهم في السادسة صباحا ومنعوا أي شخص من لدخول الى المنطقة أثناء الحدث ودمر المدرسة وسورها، والمدرسة الآن في خيمة قصة طانا لازالت مستمرة الى اليوم.

بشكل عام بعض المعلومات هناك خمس وثمانين أسير فلسطيني من بيت فوريك لازالوا يقبعون في سجون الاحتلال ومنهم أطفال ومنهم كبار في السن وهناك مئة شهيد فلسطيني من بيت فوريك وهناك عشرة شهداء تم سرقة أعضائهم ، بيت فوريك لازالت تعاني من الاحتلال وأحداث مستمرة.

وهناك قصة أخرى عن سيدة فلسطينية عمرها سبعون عام ممنوعة من زيارة ابنها في السجون تقدمت للحصول على تصريح فجاءها الرد من الإسرائيليين بأنها ممنوعة امنيا، لا نعرف ماذا يعني المنع الأمني. وهناك سيدة أخرى اعتقلها الإسرائيليون لمدة 5 سنوات وهدموا بيتها وقتلوا زوجها وخرجت من السجن منذ شهرين ....هذه هي القصص الفلسطينية ... نتمنى بان نعيش بأمان واستقرار مثل بقية شعوب العالم.

مفيدة حنني

70

Tied to a tree

demolished the tents and stole the sheep, destroying everything. They took the people out of their homes at six o'clock in the morning and prevented everyone from entering the area. They demolished the school

Beit Fureek has been suffering under the Israeli occupation since the beginning; there are lots of stories about the village. It has 12,000 people and 3 Israeli settlements: Atmar, Alon Moleh, Makhura. There is an Israeli checkpoint in the middle, between Beit Fureek and Nablus.

There are lots of stories about what has happened at this checkpoint; lots of stories about women who gave birth at the checkpoint – there have been many haemorrhages and two women have died.

My niece died in my hands when she was six years old. She had an ulcer and they stopped the ambulance from getting to her and she died with us in the car. We came back to Beit Fureek for the funeral.

There is another story about the olives and the land. Muhammad Zalmut Khatatbeh went to his land to farm his olives and some settlers came up to him and killed him. They tied him to a tree and put him on the ground with stones on top of him. Nobody knew what had happened till the next day.

Another story happened in a small village near Beit Fureek, two months ago. It is a Bedouin area with thirty-five families. The Israeli military arrived and

and its walls and the school is now in a tent. The village is called Tala and its story continues.

Just to tell you some general information; about eighty-five people have been arrested in Beit Fureek. They are now in Israeli prisons; some of them are children, some are elderly. There are a hundred Palestinian martyrs from Beit Fureek and the Israelis have stolen ten of their bodies. Beit Fureek is continually struggling against the occupation.

There is a story about one Palestinian woman, who is seventy years old, and who is not allowed to visit her son in an Israeli prison. She applied for a permit but they said to her that she has certain security points against her. We don't know what these security points mean.

There is a Palestinian woman in Beit Fureek who was taken away for five years. They demolished her house and killed her husband. She came out of prison 2 weeks ago.

These are the stories of the Palestinian area. We want security and stability like all of the people in the world.

Mofida Hanani

إقتحام

أنا أعمل فى مركز فى البلدة القديمة فى القدس جيراننا فى المركز من اليهود المتعصبين من منظمة عطروت كوهنيم، هذه المنظمة تحاول أن تجعل حياة الفلسطينيين جحيم، فهى تحاول الاستيلاء على البيوت والعقارات فى البلدة القديمة أعضاء المنظمة من أغنياء إسرائيل بحيث يسخرون المال من اجل إغراء المواطنين والاستيلاء على بيوتهم.

هناك مهندس معمارى حاول أن يتحقق فيما يفعله المستوطنين تحت المبانى فى البلدة القديمة لكن رد المستوطنين كان أن استدعوا الجنود الإسرائيليون لمنعنا من التحرك ضد ما يفعلوه.

قبل سنتين اقتحم المستوطنين مركزنا، خلال يومين حفروا فتحة فى جدار المركز ووضع فيها بوابة ودخلوا الى المركز، تفاجئنا بوجودهم يتجولون فى أملاكنا فسألناهم ماذا تفعلون هنا؟ ولماذا انتم هنا؟

ردوا أن هذا سقف بيتهم وأن لهم الحق أن نكون هنا. بعد هذة الحادثة أغلقنا الباب الذى فتح بإحكام، ولكن لم يكن بإمكاننا الذهاب الى المحكمة ومقاضاتهم.

هيام عليان، مركز السرايا القدس

72

Breaking in

I work in a centre in the old city of Jerusalem. Our neighbours at the centre are the most fanatic Israelis. They are called the Atarot Cohenim organisation. This organisation works on making the Palestinians' lives hell. They keep searching for families and houses in the old city and trying to take over houses with any sort of pressure. They are so rich that they can use any sort of influence to take over houses.

All the time in Jerusalem, settlers are digging under the ground and entering houses. In the old city now, there is an architect trying to find out what exactly they are doing under the houses there. When he asked questions, the settlers asked the soldiers to come and they stopped him from doing his work.

Two years ago they broke into our centre. Within two days, they had dug a hole in the wall and made a door; and they entered our centre. We suddenly found them walking around our property and we asked them "What are you doing here? Why you are here?"

They said "This is our roof. We have the right to be here." We closed up the door and we blocked it to try to stop them coming in but we have no other defence, we can't take them to court.

Hiyam Elayyan, Saraya Centre, Jerusalem

الاعتقال

نسا فلسطينيات معتقلات في السجون الإسرائيلية

Imprisonment

Palestinian women prisoners inside Israeli jail

حفل زفاف

لا زلت اذكر حفل الزفاف ، لم أنسى يوما ما حدث فيه.

كان ذلك حفل زفاف ابن صديقتى الزفاف كان فى الخليل وقد تزينا لبسنا أجمل الثياب، بدأ حفل الزفاف فى الساعة السابعة مساءً كان صوت الموسيقى مرتفع جداً الجميع كان يراقص العريس والعروس.

فجأة رأينا جنود إسرائيليون يدخلون الى القاعة يريدون اعتقال العريس بدأت الأم وابنتها بالبكاء والصراخ فى وجه الجنود فى محاولة لحماية العريس من الاعتقال فى حين قال احد الجنود للأم بان لا تخافى نحن نود فقط أن نسأل العريس بعض الأسئلة.

اعتقلوه لبعض الساعات قبل ان يفرجوا عنه. لكنهم أضفوا على العرس جو من الحزن بعد أن كان الجميع سعيداً، هل لكم أن تتخيلوا شعور الأم والعروس فى تلك اللحظات؟

الجميع بكوا والدموع فى أعينهم وقلوبهم محطمه.

عندما أتذكر هذه الحادثة اشعر بالتعاطف الشديد مع صديقتى، لا اعتقد أن هذا من الممكن أن يحدث مع احد فى العالم.

سارة شقيرات

Wedding party

I still remember that wedding. I have never forgotten what happened in it.

It was my friend's son's wedding. The wedding was in Hebron, and we dressed in our beautiful dresses, we were very happy. The wedding started at seven in the evening. The music was loud, everybody was dancing with bride and groom.

Suddenly we saw many soldiers coming into the hall. The soldiers

wanted to arrest the groom. The mother and her daughters began to cry and shout in the face of the soldiers to protect the son from them, but they refused.

One of them said "Don't worry, we want to ask him some questions." They arrested him for a few hours.

But after that, they changed the happiness to sadness. Can you imagine the mothers' and groom's pride and feelings at that moment? Everybody cried and left the party with tears in their eyes and with a broken heart.

When I remember that I feel such sympathy for my friend. I don't think this happens in other parts of the world.

Sarah Shqerat

حالة ولادة

ارينا متزوجة من فلسطيني ولديها طفلتان واحدة تبلغ اليوم من العمر احد عشر عام تركتها والدتها فى أوكرانيا وجاءت مع زوجها الفلسطيني لمحاولة عمل لم شمل للعائلة خلال وجودها فى فلسطين أنجبت ارينا طفلتها الثانية قبل أن تعتقل وزوجها وتصدر المحكمة الإسرائيلية على زوجها حكما بالسجن لمدة ثلاث مؤبدات. لم تكن ارينا تعرف بأى نية لزوجها او اذا ما كان يخطط للقيام بأى عمل مقاوم ضد الإحتلال.

كانت طفلتها الصغيرة معها أثناء الاعتقال وحاول الإسرائيليون أثناء التحقيق معها تهديد بطفلتها على اعتبار أن الأم من أوكرانيا فبإمكانهم إرسال طفلتها الى كيبوتس إسرائيلي كان ذلك نوع من الضغط عليها لإرغامها على إعطاء معلومات للمخابرات الإسرائيلية. لقد تعرضت للتعذيب والضغط والضرب.

أما عن الطفلة التى فى أوكرانيا فلم تتمكن من زيارة أمها او حتى التحدث إليها، ولم تسمح السفارة الإسرائيلية فى أوكرانيا للطفلة الحضور لزيارة الأم. كان هناك محاولات عديدة للزيارة لكن الإسرائيليون كانوا على الدوام يرفضون.

الطفلة الموجودة فى فلسطين هى الوحيدة التى تستطيع زيارة والدتها ووالدها، هى تذهب لزيارة ألام الموجودة فى سجن هشارون كل أسبوعين مثلا او كل شهر، وكذلك تزور الأب الموجود فى سجن نفحة، كم تبعد نفحة عن مخيم الدهيشة

حيث تعيش وكم تبعد الدهيشة عن هشارون. المعاناة كبيرة لهذه الطفلة التى تصحو فى الساعة الثالثة والنصف او الرابعة صباحا لأجل أن تستعد وتذهب مع جدتها او جدها لزيارة والدها أو والدتها، وتتعرض للتفتيش والحواجز الكثيرة.

حتى زيارة الأزواج المعتقلين غير مسموحه، هذا جزء بسيط من معاناة الأسيرات خاصة الأمهات وتحديداً للعائلات التى فيها الزوجين داخل المعتقل. صورة الأسيرة سمر صبيح وهى مقيدة بأيديها وأرجلها على مرأى وسمع كل العالم حتى تلفزيون العربية صورها قبل دخولها الى غرفة الولادة بساعتين وقد كنت موجودة رأيتها عندما أحضرت ونزلت من السيارة لأنى كنت أعرف موعد الولادة.

لقد تمكنا فى مؤسسة منديلا وبعد صراع فى المحكمة العليا الإسرائيلية من استصدار قرار يسمح بفك القيود من أيدى وأرجل المعتقلات أثناء الولادة، حيث كانت عملية الولادة تتم واليدين مكبلتين مثل ما حصل مع الأسيرات ميرفت طه ومنال غانم كلاهما كانتا مكبلات بالسرير عند الولادة.

الحمد لله فى هذا الوقت لا يوجد أطفال داخل السجن ونتمنى ألا يحصل. طبعا أعداد الأسرى الموجودين اليوم فى السجون تقريبا تسعة آلاف ولا تستطيع تحديد الرقم لأن عمليات الاعتقال مستمرة.

طبعا هناك عدد من الأسرى الإداريون هم معتقلين بدون توجيه أى تهم لهم.

بثينة دوقماق

78

Having a baby

A Ukrainian woman and her Palestinian husband are in prison. Her husband is in prison for three life sentences. They have a daughter, who is eleven years old and who lives in the Ukraine. They met in Ukraine and the girl was born there. The woman returned to Palestine and gave birth to another daughter and was imprisoned when her daughter was small. She was imprisoned with her husband and did not know what her husband was up to, whatever it was. Her charge was because she was his wife.

The Israelis used the second daughter to threaten her. As the mother was from Russia they said they would put the daughter in a kibbutz, if she did not give them information. That created terror and pressure for her. The second daughter is actually still with her grandmother.

Moreover, the girl in the Ukraine can neither visit nor talk to her mother. The Israeli Embassy did not allow the daughter or her grandmother, who both live in the Ukraine, to visit. They tried many times. Only the daughter inside Palestine can visit her mother. She visited her mother, in Hasharon prison, and her father in Nafha prison, every two weeks or a month. The jails were far apart. The girl suffered a lot, waking at 3 or 4 in the morning to go with the grandmother and grandfather through many checkpoints. The girl now in Ukraine can't even visit her parents once every three months. She can't even make a phone call to them. This is a simple part of the suffering of the women prisoners, especially if their husbands are in jail as well.

Another example of this is prisoner Samar Speh. Her photo was shown on television to the whole world when her hands and legs were tied – every one could see and hear her on Arabic television two hours before she gave birth. I was there and saw her when she came out of the police car: I was there because I knew when she was due to give birth. We managed at Mandela* after a struggle in the Israeli Supreme Court to get a decision that women could be released from handcuffs when they were going to give birth. Because in the past, women gave birth with their hands tied to the bed, as happened for Marfat Taha and Manal Ghanam.

At 10 o'clock in the morning Samar arrived at the hospital and at twelve o'clock she gave birth. The child is still with his mother and if she remains in prison for two years the child will stay with her. If the mother is in prison for longer than this, the child will leave the prison and the mother will remain, as happened to Manal Ghanam. The mother is still in prison. Thank God there are no children in prison at the moment; we hope this never happens again.

The total number of prisoners is around nine thousand. It cannot be calculated exactly as people go in and out daily.

Buthaina Duqmaq

* Mandela-Palestine Society

فقدان أولادي

مع بدأ الانتفاضة الأولى كان عبد المنعم يدرس بجامعة بير زيت فاغتالته قوة إسرائيلية خاصة أطلقوا النار عليه عدد من الرصاصات أصابه وجهه أثناء عودته من المسجد الأقصى حيث كان يصلي. بعد مقتله انخرط كل أبنائي في مقاومة الاحتلال بعنف فاعتقل الإسرائيليون أربعة منهم وهدموا بيتنا لأول مرة.

اعتقل ابني ناصر وحكم تسعة مؤبدات وخمسين عام وبعد ذلك شقيقة نصر حكم خمسة مؤبدات وثلاثين عام، ثم جاء دور شريف فحكم أربعة مؤبدات وبعده محمد حكم ثلاثة مؤبدات وثلاثين سنة. إبني إسلام حكم لمدة خمس سنوات ونصف ودفع غرامة عشرة آلاف شيكل، وجهاد اعتقل لمدة سنتين وباسل لمدة أربع سنين وتكرر هدم بيتنا بعد ذلك مرتين، نحن نعيش اليوم في بيت إبني المعتقل ناصر للأسف لا يوجد لنا بيت خاص.

أولادي الأربعة في السجن منذ ثماني سنوات ومنذ خمس سنوات لم يسمح لي بزيارتهم.

منذ اعتقال أبنائي أصبح أبوهم ضرير ....

رغم الأسر ورغم هدم البيوت فنحن والحمد لله صامدين وسنظل نناضل ونقاوم حتى نعيد ما سلبه الاحتلال.

ام عبد المنعم

عندي عشرة أبناء وبنتين كانوا أطفال ربيتهم تربية جيدة وعلمتهم رغم صعوبة الحياة، وسياسات الاحتلال وإجراءات القمع التي يمارسها، أنهى معظم أبنائي دراسة التوجيهي.

عند بدأ إنتفاضة الأقصى بسبب دخول الحقير أريئيل شارون للمسجد الأقصى وتدنيسه، إنخرط الشباب في مقاومة الاحتلال البعض منهم أكمل تعليمه والبعض الآخر قاوم إنضم للعمل النضالي ضد الاحتلال، هذا واجب علينا جميعاً أن نقاوم من استولى على أرضنا وأخذ كل شيء، ودنس مقدساتنا وصادر حريتنا.

أول أولادي عبد المنعم تعرض للاعتقال وهو في سن الثانية عشر ودخل المعتقل حكم ستة أشهر وبعد خروجه تغيرت حياته كلياً وانخرط في صفوف العمل الوطني لمقاومة الاحتلال.

Losing my children

I have ten sons and two daughters. I educated them when they were children – I educated them although it was very difficult with the Israeli policies and the violence around us. Most of my children finished their Towjehi [high school certificate].

The Al Aqsa Intifada started because the despicable Sharon entered the Al-Aqsa Mosque and disgraced it. Then the Intifada started and the youth started to resist the Occupation. Some of them continued their studies and some chose to resist the Occupation because of what was imposed upon us. It was our duty to resist people who took our lands and took our land and holy places – it took everything. That took everything from us. We did not go to the Occupation; the Occupation came to us.

My first son was Abed al-Munem. He was arrested when he was twelve years old. He was inside for six months. When he came out of prison, his whole life was changed and he was involved in resisting the occupation.

During the first Intifada my son studied in Birzeit University. The Special Forces assassinated him. They shot many bullets in his face after he returned from prayer at the Al Aqsa Mosque. After he was killed, all of my children got involved in the resistance.

His brothers started to violently resist the occupation. Four of them were arrested and our house was destroyed for the first time.

Naaser was arrested and he was given nine life sentences and fifty years in prison. His brother Nassr was given five life sentences and thirty years. Shareef was given four life sentences, Mohammed was given three life sentences and thirty years. Islam was given five and a half years and fined ten thousand shekels. Jihad was given two years; and Basil was given four years.

They destroyed our house two times. Now we live in Naaser's house. Unfortunately, we don't have a house of our own and my children have been in prison for eight years. For five years I have been unable to visit them.

After my children were arrested, their father became blind.

Although many have been arrested and many houses have been destroyed, we are still steadfast. Thank God we keep resisting, until we can take back everything from the Occupation.

Um Abed Al-Munem

في انتظار ابنها

عاشوا معاً الحياة حلوها ومرها أنشئوا أبناءهم على الكرامة والانتماء وحب الخير والعطاء، لم يكونوا يعلموا أن هذا سيعود عليهم بالألم في المستقبل وان كان هذا الألم واقعاً فهو الم أمة بأكملها.

كان في أمي هو شيء من التمرد وقادرة على قول الحق مهما كلفها، وكانت امرأة طيبة وقوية وجميل أن تكون هذه الصفات في إنسانه، وكان عند أبي إصرار وحكمة وهدوء يشوبه الحذر وهذا ما ورثناه منهم.

هكذا انشأ الأبناء بهذه الصفات وبانتمائهم للوطن وحب العطاء كأي أبناء فلسطين، أصبح لأمي ابن سجين وآخر مطارد من قبل الإسرائيليون لا يعلم إلا الله أين هو.

قالت أمي : أم صالح: سهرت ليالي طويلة ، وفي ليالي الشتاء اجلس خلف النافذة انظر الى الأفق من خلال

المطر المنهمر لعلي المح خيال يطمئنني على ابني المطارد او أن يكون قد اختلس دقائق ليعود الى المنزل ليرى والديه، لكن كان البيت دائما تحت مراقبة الجيش حتى اذا ما اعتقلوه.

كم مضى عليها أيام مسافرة من سجن الى سجن تجوب الوطن شماله لجنوبه تبحث عن ابنها السجين عن أخباره دون أن تعلم شيء، وكم بكت وفقدت متعة النوم وأي نكه للطعام، وأي شعور بالفرحة وكان المعنى الوحيد الذي تمسكت به وأبقته أمام أعينها والذي من أجله فقدت أي معنى اخر هو الحرية والكرامة الذي من اجله شرد ابنائها وسجنوا وحرموا من النوم وعذبوا.

وهذا حال كل الأمهات الفلسطينيات اللاتي ينظرن لغد مشرق لهن ولأبنائهن طال انتظار صباحه، وأم صالح تتحدث بلسان الأمهات جميعاً أمهات أنهكهن التعب وتحول الى مرض أقعدهن الفراش حتى فارقن الحياة مرهقات من الظروف المحيطة بهن وأمي زريفة داوود (أم صالح) كانت أحداهن رحمها الله.

نجاح عياد

Waiting for her son

They lived life together, bringing up their children in dignity, with kindness, love and a giving nature. They didn't know that this would return to them in the future as pain or that this pain would affect the whole nation.

My mother had rebellion in her and she told the truth at all costs. She was a strong, kind and good-looking woman. These are beautiful in a human being. My father was persistent, wise, calm and cautious. These are the qualities that we inherited from them.

They brought up their children with these characteristics and with a sense of belonging to their land and a love of giving. This was like all the children of Palestine. One of my mother's sons became a prisoner but they were not told where, and another was wanted by the Israelis – only God knows where he is now.

My mother (Um Salih) said: "I stayed up late at night and in the winter nights I sat behind the window, looking out at the horizon through the pouring rain. I used to try to imagine that my missing son was well, or dream that he could steal some minutes to come home and see his father and mother. But the house was always watched by the Israelis so even if he came home they would capture him."

How many days she spent travelling from prison to prison, scouring the country north and south searching for her imprisoned son or for any news of him, never knowing anything. How much she cried and how much sleep she lost, losing her appetite too and any sense of joy.

Freedom and dignity were the only thing she held on to and she kept them in front of her eyes always. It was for freedom and dignity that her children were away from her: it was for that that they were imprisoned, kept without sleep and subjected to torture.

This is the situation of all Palestinian mothers who look towards a bright tomorrow for themselves and for their children, waiting for the dawn to come.

Um Salih speaks for every mother, tired and ill from exhaustion, who passes away due to the circumstances around them.

My mother, Zareefeh Dawood [Um Salih] was one of them.

Najah Ayyad

مفــصــولين

Separation

البريطانيون كانوا سيئين، لقد كذبوا علينا، إمتدت فترة الانتداب البريطاني في فلسطين لسنوات، لم نستطع فعل شيء، لم يعطونا أي فرصة، من قال أنهم جيدون؟ لقد أعطوا أرضنا لليهود، لم نرى السعادة بعد الانتداب البريطاني.

عندما كان البريطانيون موجودين هنا، قام اليهود بوضع قنابل في باب العامود لقتل الأبرياء، كنت هناك عندما حدثت الانفجارات، يقولون على الدوام أن الفلسطينيون إرهابيون، وأنا أتسأل من هو الإرهابي؟

والآن هم يرددون على الدوام أن من حق إسرائيل حماية نفسها، بلد بجيش ودبابات يحاولون حماية أنفسهم من شعب أعزل إلا من الحجارة؟ أي أذى من الممكن أن نلحقه بهم؟

والآن الجدار الإسرائيلي لقد جعلونا نجوب الحقول والحدائق من أجل أن نصل الى مدينة القدس، لقد وصلنا مناطق لم نكن لنصلها لأن الشوارع كانت مغلقة، كان علينا أن نتسلق الجدران ونقفز عنها من أجل الوصول، لقد منعونا من الذهاب الى القدس، أخذوا أرضنا وأصبحنا غرباء فيها، جعلونا نتجول كل الوقت وفي كل الاتجاهات من أجل الوصول الى القدس.

لقد أصبحنا بحاجة الى من يدلنا على الطرق والشوارع المؤدية الى المدينة، إن الوصول الى مدينة القدس أشبه برحلتي الأخيرة الى الأردن فانا لم اذهب الى الأردن منذ زمن طويل وكنت قد مررت بها في طريقي الى السعودية لتأدية مراسم الحج. لم أتمكن من إيجاد طريقي في الأردن، كما أنا اليوم لا أستطيع أن أجد طريقي في القدس.

الحجة عريفة

The City

They are really bad the British, they set us up and lied to us. The British Mandate stretched on for years – what could we do – they did not give us any opportunity. Who says they are good? They gave our land away to the Jews. We can never be happy since the British time.

When the British were there, the Jews put bombs at Damascus Gate. They killed people. I was there when that happened. They keep saying the Palestinians are terrorists. Who are the terrorists?

And now, they are saying all the time that the Israelis are protecting themselves. A people who have an army and tanks have to protect themselves from people who have only stones? What can we do to them?

Now this Israeli Wall - We have to go all through the fields in order to reach Jerusalem. We reach areas we will never reach because the streets are blocked. We have to climb over fields or jump over a wall. We are forbidden to go to Jerusalem, the land stopped being our land, we were foreigners in our land. All the time we are travelling around and around, we did not leave a wall that we did not jump from or a garden that we did not walk through to get to Jerusalem.

We need someone to show us the way to get there and to show us the streets. It is like a journey to Jordan, I had not been there for many years, so when I went there passing through to Haj, I did not know my way around. It is similar now when I go to Jerusalem, I cannot find my way around.

Hajeh Arifeh, aged about 85 years

البحر

استيقظ فى الصباح الباكر وأرى شروق الشمس، أرى منظرا جميل عند الشروق، أرى سطح البحر الميت وهو يلمع مع الشروق والشمس تشرق من خلف مستوطنة معالى ادوميم وهى مستوطنة إسرائيلية انظر إليها فأرى منظرها كالتمساح.

وأنا انظر الى شروق الشمس أقول قد يكون غدا أفضل لكن عندما التفت من حولى أجد الجدار يلتف من حولنا اشعر بألم شديد وأشبه حياتنا بعلبة السردين وأفكر فى مستقبل الشباب ماذا سيجدون غدا غير المأساة والعذاب والحصار، سيحبطون.

وهذه مأساة الشعب الفلسطينى بالرغم من أنى اسكن فى مكان جميل ومنظر باهر لكن الجدار يشوهه.

أرأيتم كم هذا مؤلم ؟

أرأيتم العذاب الذى يعيشه الشعب الفلسطينى ؟

ماذا سيجد أطفالنا غدا ؟

حكمت حمدان

أنا أصلاً من بلدةٍ ساحليةٍ اسمها بورنموث، كان البحر مهماً جداً لنا، أتذكر خلال الحرب العالمية الثانية، لقد وضعوا أسلاك شائكة لمنعنا من .

الوصول الى البحر. أتذكر كم كنت مستاءةً من فكرةِ عدم تمكنى من الوصول الى البحر، كنت فعلا أفتقد البحر.

بالعودةِ الى الماضى،لم يدم إغلاق البحر فترة طويلةً.

من سيدةٍ بريطانيا فى رد فعلها لقصص النساء الفلسطينيات بوصف جدار الفصل.

88

The sea

I see a beautiful view when I wake up in the early morning. When the sun rises, from my roof I see the Dead Sea, gleaming in the dawn. And when the sun rises opposite the settlement of Maale Adumim – an Israeli settlement – I see it like a crocodile.

And as I watch the sun rise, I say that maybe there will be a promise of a better tomorrow, and when I see the Wall, winding around us, I feel an acute pain, and I liken our life to a wrapped-around tin of sardines, and I think of the future of the young people. Will they find a tomorrow without tragedy and pain and siege, and will they be depressed?

And this is the tragedy of the Palestinian people. Although I live in a place with a stunning view, the Wall spoils its beauty.

Can you see how this is painful?

Can you see the pain that the Palestinian people live in?

What tomorrow will our children find?

Hikmat Hamdan

I come from Bournemouth which is by the sea and the sea is very important to us.

I remember during the Second World War, they put barbed wire up and stopped us going to the sea.

I remember how bad I felt when I couldn't go there, I really missed it.

When I look back I realise that we weren't cut off from the sea for very long.

Comment by a British woman in reaction to the Palestinian women's stories of the Separation Wall

89

كيف ناضلت والدتي من أجل حياة أخي. عندما كنت فى الثانية، ولد أخي مع خلل فى القلب خطير للغاية، وقال الأطباء لوالدتي أن تدعوه، لأن طفلها لن يعيش بعد هذا اليوم. أخذت أمي الطفل إلى المستشفى حيث كان الأطباء الذين يمكن أن يساعدوا فى شفائه. سافرت الى المستشفى متنقلةً بين حافلتين صغيرتين، ورحلة القطار كانت تغادر فجرا، وتعود ليلا.

قال الأطباء أن أخي قد لا يرى السنة الأولى من حياته، ولكن أمي لم تقبل بهذا. ذهبت لإيصاله الى هذا المستشفى يوما بعد يوم، ثم أسبوعا بعد أسبوع ، لمدةٍ تسع سنوات كانت تحمله على ظهرها، على اثنين من تلك الحافلات والقطار، حتى أصبح قويا بما فيه الكفاية للخضوع لعملية جراحيةٍ يمكن أن تشفيه بشكل دائم. أمي قد وعدت ابنها بالحياة، وليس الحكومة التى بنت المستشفيات فى المناطق التى كان يسكنها بيض، كان من الصعب الحصول على نفس الراعية فى الضواحى التى يسكنها السود. اليوم يبلغ أخي (49)عاما، وهو والد لطفلين .

عندما كانت أمى 23 تزوجت من رجل وفى بوعوده ، لها ولأطفالها. كان عنيدا وقد قطع عهدا على نفسه وعلى شعبه لمكافحة التمييز العنصري. أمي ساعدته فى الحفاظ على هذا الوعد. معا ربوا وأنشئوا أربعةُ مقاتلين مناوئين لنظام الفصل العنصري، ولكن تلك قصة أخرى. أحد هؤلاء الأطفال أبعد للمنفى من قبل حكومةُ الفصل العنصري فى جنوب أفريقيا لقد كنت أنا. والدتي وعدت بأنها ستكون دائما هناك عندما كنت بحاجةٍ لها. وقبل بضع سنوات ، ابنتي مرضت، اقترضت أمي المال للسفر جوا، سافرت على متن الطائرة الاولى التى يمكن أن تحصل عليها، لتكون إلى جانبي. كانتْ تبلغ اثنتين وسبعين عاماً لكنها حتى الآن لم تكسر وعداً قطعته لي.

بعد ذلك بسنتين ، عندما كانت أمى قد بلغت الرابعةُ والسبعين، تعرض والدي لسكتةُ دماغيةٍ حادة. الحكومة الجديدة، بعد انتهاء الفصل العنصري وعدت وعودا كثيرة، بما فى ذلك الوعود الى الشيوخ والمرضى والفقراء بأنها سوف ستقوم بالاعتناء بهم. والداى قد وفيا بوعدهما فى الكفاح من أجل تحرير جنوب أفريقيا، ولكن الحكومة الجديدة لم تلتزم بوعودها لهم. المستشفى الذى أخذت والدتي والدي إليه أعاده الى المنزل ليموت. والدتي لن تدعه يموت، على مدار السنوات الخمس الماضية، مع مساعدة من بعض الأشخاص الذين كانت قد حافظت على وعودها لهم، والدتي كانت قادرة على الحفاظ على زواجها ووعودها لزوجها – أن تحبه وتعتنى به دائماً.

حتى اليوم، لا تزال والدتي تحافظ على وعودها، ولا تزال تغنى عندما تطهو وتنظف وتغسل وتكوى الملابس، وترعى بيتها والأسرة. هذه هى ذكرياتي من والدتي.

شرين بندت [بريطانيا]

سيكون لدينا تعليم جيد وأصبحنا معلمين، ومحاسب، ومحام. أحيانا حفظ تلك الوعود يعنى الخروج للعمل عندما كنا فى المدرسة، أو الجلوس فى المخبز ليلا أو الخياطة لأموال إضافية. ولكن والدتي كانت امرأةً ولها كلمة، كلمةً لم تكن تنقطع أبدا. ولا فى الأشياء الصغيرة ولا فى الأمور الكبيرة.

واحدة من ذكرياتى الأولى الصغيرة، هو الذهاب إلى الشاطئ مع والدى، لم يكن لدينا سيارة ذهبنا بالقطار إلى شاطئ كان والدى يتذكره من طفولته، عندما وصلنا الى هناك لم يسمح لنا بدخول الى الشاطئ. كان قد أعلن هذا الشاطئ للبيض فقط، وكانت هناك علامات لهذا الغرض فى كل مكان، عاد والدى بنا الى المنزل بالقطار مجددا.

بعد كل شىء، كنا اثنتين من الفتيات الصغيرات، وصبيا مريضا كانوا يضطرون الى حمله وطفل رضيع، ولكن قد وعدت أمى أولادها فى نزهة على الشاطئ، وفعلا قام كل منهما بحمل اثنين منا -- والدى حمل سلة النزهةُ أيضا – حملونا لأميال عديدةٍ إلى أن وصلنا إلى جزء من الشاطئ الذى كان يسمح لنا باستخدامه. كانت تتناثر فيها الأقماض والصخور وهو السبب وراء ترك الشاطئ مفتوحاً لنا، بالكاد وصلنا هناك، قبل أن تجرح شقيقتي قدمها، ذهبنا جميعا الى المستشفى لكى يخيطوا لها جرحها، جلسنا فى المستشفى طول اليوم.

والدتى لم تنس وعدها لنا، أمضت كل ليلةُ فى حياكةُ الملابس للآخرين لدفع ثمن الرحلة الثانية للتنزه وغيرها كثير. لا حكومة الفصل العنصري ولا جرح أختى على الشاطئ، والذى كان علامةُ من الرب، منع أمى من الحفاظ والوفاء بوعودها لأولادها.

واحد من الأشياء الكبيرة، والذى هو أسطورةُ فى عائلتنا، هو

وعود

قصةٌ من جنوب أفريقيا خلال الحكم العنصرى

حياة أمى كانت حياة واعدة.

مثل كل والدةٍ كانت والدتى جميلة، طاهية رائعة، مميزة بخبز الكعك، لقد كانت خياطتها أشبه بالحلم، كانت تحترم وتقدر والدتها وتحب زوجها وأولادها بعشق ، والأحفاد وأبناء الأحفاد. فى هذا الحب، هى مثل كل الأمهات.

إهتمت والدتى بجيرانها والأقارب وعادت المرضى، إعتنت بأطفالهم عندما لا يستطيعون وقامت بالطهى والتنظيف، كل هذه الأمور تشاركها أمى مع ملايين من الأمهات والزوجات والبنات والجيران الطيبين.

كانت لأمى ميزتان كنت أحبهما، أولهما حفاظها على وعودها والآخر هو امتلاكها لصوت رائع فى الغناء. كبرنا مع صوت غناء أمى فى حين كانت تجهز وتنظف وتعلق الغسيل ليجف، كنا نتغذى وعود وأحلام والدتى. ولكن حياة والدتى لم تكن دائما من أجل الغناء، فحياتها الخاصة عرفت حالات من الوعود والأحلام المحطمة.

حتى بلغت سن الرابعة، كانت والدتى تستمع الى القصص من والدها وهى تجلس على ركبته وغنت مع فرقته على خشبة المسرح، وكانت والدتى درة عينه.

فى يوم ما غادر والدها ، مع وعد بأن يعود. أمى انتظرت وقتا طويلا لـ»يوما ما«، لم يأت ذلك أبدا، الشيء الآخر الذى لم يأت، كان الطعام. جدتى كانت أمية ولم تكن تتكلم لغة بلد زوجها. وكان لديها أربعة أطفال صغار.

لم يكن من السهل فى تلك الأيام لمثل هذه المرأة العثور على عمل ليس مثل اليوم. فى البداية عندما استيقظ أطفالها وطلبوا الطعام، قامت جدتى بإنزال الستائر وقالت لهم أن يخلدوا الى النوم ، لم يأت الموعد لتناول الإفطار بعد، الأمر الذى إستمر لفترة طويلة، فعلى الرغم من مشاهدة والدتى لنور الشمس يتسلل عبر الستائر، إلا أن جدتى كانت تصر أن الليل لم يزل بعد، فى نهاية المطاف توقف الأطفال عن طلب الطعام من جدتى.

قامت جدتى بوضع والدتى وأخوتها فى ملجأ للأيتام، لأنها لم تتمكن من توفير الطعام لهم ووعدت بالعودة «يوما ما» عندما تجد وظيفة وبيت يأويهم معا مرة أخرى.

إنتظرت أمى وقتا طويلا لـ»يوما ما« على أمل عودة جدتى مرة أخرى، لم يشعر أخوة وأخوات والدتى بالراحة فى الملجأ، حيث كان يتم فصل الفتيات عن الأولاد فى بداية فترة إقامتهم فى دار للأيتام.

كل ليلة كان يتم فصل والدتى عن أختها الأكبر، حيث كان يتم فصل الفتيات حسب العمر، بين قسم البنات الكبيرات حيث كانت شقيقة والدتى والأصغر سنا حيث كانت والدتى، كان خط السكك الحديدية على السقف، ليحمل الستائر المصنوعة من الجلود التى كانت معلقة على القضبان الحديدية.

أسوأ ذكرى لوالدتى حينها لم تكن تعرضها للضرب على أيدى الراهبات اللواتى كن يدرن دار الأيتام، ولا السرير البارد والثابت أو عدم كفاية الغذاء، كانت الذكرى هى تلك الستائر الجلدية التى كانت تفصل بينها وبين الشخص الوحيد الذى تبقى لها فى سن الرابعة أختها الكبرى، والدتى تتذكر رنين الحلقات المعدنية الحاملة للستار على طول القضبان المعدنية، الخوف من الحرمان والشعور بالتخلى عنهم. حتى يومنا هذا والدتى لا تستطيع تحمل صوت إسدال الستائر على الحلقات المعدنية على طول السكة الحديدية الحاملة للستائر.

فى نهاية المطاف، جاءت جدتى وأخذت أمى وإخوتها، لم تكن جدتى تبحث عن مجرد وظيفة ومنزل، بل قالت أنها تريد أيضا العثور على زوج جديد، وبالفعل تزوجت المزارع الذى كانت تعمل لديه. جدتى كانت مسلمةً من أصل الملايو، وكان زوجها غير المسلم من أصل أوروبى. هذا كان أمرا مستهجنا، ولكن كان شرعيا فى زيمبابوى فى تلك الأيام.

السنوات التى عاشوها فى مزرعة زوج أمها كانت الأيام الأجمل أيام الطفولة لأنه كان يعاملها هى وأشقاؤها كأولاد له.

كل شيء انتهى عندما كان عمر والدتى فى الثالثة عشرة، كان ذلك عندما عادت جدتى، ولها الآن ستة أطفال، لزيارةِ والديها فى مدينة كيب تاون فى مسقط رأسها فى جنوب أفريقيا، لم يذهب زوج أمها معهم. لعائلة جنوب أفريقيا ولا حكومة جنوب أفريقيا وافقت على الزواج من زوج جدتى. والدى جدتى لم يسمحوا لها بالعودة إلى زوجها الجديد، الحكومة لن تسمح له بالانضمام إليها. حكومة جنوب أفريقيا على وشك أن تجعل من غير الشرعى لجدتى العيش تحت سقف واحد مع زوجها، ناهيك عن تقاسم السرير معه.

علقت جدتى فى كيب تاون من دون زوجها، ولا يوجد أى وسيلة للعودة إليه. السبيل الوحيد للبقاء على قيد الحياة لجدتى وأطفالها، كان بإرسال الأطفال الأكبر سنا للعمل والدتى عملت فى مصنع جنبا إلى جنب مع أشقائها الكبار كانوا يعملون حتى الساعة الثانية عشر ليلا. كانت والدتى فتاةً ذكية كتبت إلى زوج أمها لتطلب منه أن يحضرهم له، وجاء الرد واعدا بأنه سيبذل كل جهده لكى يعيدهم يوم من الأيام أمى كانت تنتظر إلى الأبد «يوما ما».

لم تكن والدتى لتعرف حتى بعد سنوات، مدى الصعوبة التى واجهها زوج أمها محاولاً العثور عليهم، وكيف أن العديد من العقبات وضعِت فى طريقها، حتى عاد أخيراً ليموت فى مزرعته، وحيداً، حزيناً.

لقد نشأت والدتى مع أم لم تخلف وعودا قطعتها لأولادها أبدا. وعدت بأننا لن نجوع، ونحن لم نجع بعد ذلك أبدا. وعدت لن نكون بلا مأوى، وفعلا لم نكن يوما بدون مأوى. وعدت أنه

91

Promises

a story from South Africa

My mother's life has been one of promises.

Like everyone's mother, my mother is beautiful. She's a great cook. She bakes wonderful cakes. She sews like a dream. She honoured her mother, loves her husband and adores her children, grandchildren and great-grandchildren. In these ways too, she is like all mothers. My mother has cared for the ailing parents of her neighbours and relatives, looked after their kids when they couldn't and cooked and cleaned for them when they were ill. All these things, my mother shares with millions of other mothers, wives, daughters and good neighbours.

Two things set my mother apart. One is her approach to promises. The other is her great singing voice. We grew up with the sound of our mother singing, while she cooked and cleaned and hung up washing to dry. We were nurtured on my mother's promises. But my mother's life wasn't always one for singing about and her own life was littered with broken promises.

Until she was four, my mother listened to stories on her father's knee and sang with his band on stage and was generally the apple of his eye. Then one day he left, with a promise that he'd be back someday. My mother waited a long time for "someday". It never came. The other thing which didn't come, was food. My mother's mother – my gran - was illiterate. Gran didn't speak the language of her husband's country. She had four young children. It wasn't easy in those days for such a woman to find work. It isn't today. At first when her children woke and asked for food, my gran would draw the curtains and tell them to go to sleep, it wasn't time for breakfast yet. That went on for a long time. My mum remembers how often she could see the sun peeping beneath and around the curtains, yet still my gran said it was night, not time to eat. Eventually the children stopped asking. Fearing that they'd never wake up and ask for food again, my gran put my mum and her siblings into an orphanage. She promised to come back 'some day' when she had a job and home for them again. My mother waited a long time for 'someday' when my gran would return. Her siblings were no comfort,

because the girls had been separated from the boys at the beginning of their stay at the orphanage. Every night my mother would be separated from her older sister. Between the section for older girls where her sister slept and that for younger ones, was a metal rail set in the ceiling, from which a leather curtain hung on iron rails. My mother's worst memory of that time isn't the beatings by the nuns who ran the orphanage, the cold hard beds or the inadequate food. It is the drawing of curtains every night between her and the only person she had left in her four-year old world. My mother remembers the ringing of metal curtain rings along metal rails as the sound of deprivation, loss and abandonment. To this day, she cannot abide the sound of curtains drawn on metal rings along a metal rail.

My mother and her siblings were eventually fetched by my gran. Gran hadn't just found a job and a home, she'd also found a new husband. She'd married the farmer she'd been working for. My grandmother was a Muslim of Malay descent. Her husband was a non-Muslim of European descent. This was frowned on, but not illegal in Zimbabwe in those days. The years on her stepfather's farm were the greatest days of my mother's childhood because he was a kind man who treated her and her siblings as his own.

It all ended when my mother was thirteen. That was when my grandmother returned, with her now six children, to visit her parents in Cape Town in her native South Africa. My mother's stepfather didn't go with them. Neither Gran's family nor the South African government approved of marriages like hers. Gran's parents wouldn't let her return to her new husband. The government wouldn't let him join her. The South African government was about to make it illegal for Gran to live under the same roof as her husband, let alone share a bed with him.

My gran was now stuck in Cape Town without her husband, illiterate and penniless, with no way to get back to him. The only way for Gran to survive was to put her older children to work. So at thirteen my mother, together with her older siblings, started work in a factory. She was a bright girl, though, my mother. She'd written to her stepfather to ask him to fetch them. He'd written back, promising that he would, someday. My mother waited forever for 'someday'. My mother wasn't to know, until years later, how hard her stepfather had tried to find them and how many obstacles had been put in his way, until he finally went back to die on his farm, alone and heartbroken.

I grew up with a mother who never broke promises to her children. She promised that we would never go hungry and we never did. She promised that we would never be homeless and we never were. She promised we would have a good education and we became teachers, an accountant, a lawyer. Sometimes keeping those promises meant her going out to work when we were at school, or sitting up at night baking or sewing for extra money. But my mother was a woman of her word and her word to her children was never broken. Not in small things. Not in big things.

One of my earliest memories of the little things is of being taken to the beach by my parents. We didn't have a car. We went by train to a beach my father remembered from his childhood. When we got there, we weren't allowed on the beach. It had been declared for whites only and there were signs to that effect everywhere. My parents could have got back on the train and gone home. After all, they had two little girls, a sickly boy who had to be carried and an infant. But my mother had promised her children a picnic on the beach. So she and my dad each carried two of us – my dad the picnic basket also – for miles until we came to a part of the beach that we were allowed to use. It was strewn with debris and pointed rocks which is why whites didn't want it. We were barely there, when my sister cut her foot. We all trooped off to the hospital to have it stitched. We sat at the hospital all day, until the foot was stitched and the picnic food all eaten. My mother didn't forget her promise to us. She spent every night sewing clothes for other people to pay for a second trip and for many other outings. Not the apartheid government with its whites only signs nor the good lord with his pointed rocks would keep her from fulfilling her promise to her children.

One of the big things, which is legend in our family, is how my mother fought for my brother's life. When I was two, my brother was born with a very serious heart defect. Doctors told my mother to call the imam and name him, because he wouldn't live out the day. My mother called the imam and named her son. Then she took him to a hospital where there were doctors who could see to him. She travelled to that hospital on two buses and one train and she travelled back home to her

other children on two buses and one train. She left at dawn and returned at night. Doctors said he'd not see his first year of life, but my mother would not accept this. She went on taking him to that hospital, day after day, then week after week, for nine years, carrying him on her back, on those two buses and a train going, two buses and a train coming home again, until finally he was strong enough for the operation which could heal him permanently. My mother had promised her son the gift of life. Not the government which built hospitals in white areas which were hard to get to from black townships, nor the good lord who created her child with a heart defect, could stop my mother fulfilling that promise. Today my brother is 49 and the father of two children.

When my mother was 23 she married a man who kept promises, to her and their children. The thing was, he'd also made a promise to himself and his people to fight apartheid. My mother helped him keep that promise. Together they raised four anti-apartheid fighters, but that's another story. One of those children went into exile from apartheid South Africa. That was me. My mother promised that she would always be there when I needed her. A few years ago, my daughter fell seriously ill. My mother borrowed airfare and flew over on the first plane she could get, to be by my side. She was seventy-two but she had never yet broken a promise to me.

Two years later, when my mother was seventy-four, my dad had a severe stroke. The new, post-apartheid government had made many promises, including promises that the old and the sick and the poor would be cared for. My parents had kept their promise to fight for a free South Africa, but the new government didn't keep its promises to them. The hospital which my mother took my dad to, sent him home to die. My mother took him home, but she would not let him die. For the past five years, with the help of some of the people to whom she had kept promises all her life, my mother has been able to keep her marriage promise to her husband – to love him and care for him.

So, today, my mother still keeps promises. And still she sings – when she cooks and cleans and washes and irons and looks after her home and family. These are my enduring memories of my mother.

Shireen Pandit [UK]

رانية وماهر

والداى عاشا فى قرية العيسوية، الأم بثينة والأب موسى واجهوا نفس الظروف التى مر بها العاشقين روميو وجوليت واستمر حبهم لعشر سنوات جدى وجدتى لم يحضرا الزواج ولكن خالتى حضرت ولما عادت الى المنزل ضربها جدى وسجنها فى غرفة النوم، كانت المشكلة الأكبر أن الجيش جاء واعتقل والدى يوم الزفاف، حيث أن المشاركة السياسية كانت ممنوعة وتم اعتقال 30 شخص من العائلة، خرج بعد فترة وأنجبا 4 أولاد وبنتان ومن ثم اعتقال لمدة أربع سنوات أخرى لأسباب سياسة وبعدها خرج وأنجبا ثلاث فتيات أخريات وبعدها سجن لأنه ينتمى الى منظمة فتح

وفى هذا الوقت كنت طالبة خدمة إجتماعية فى جامعة القدس، كنت أزور والدى فى السجن كل ثلاث أشهر، وهذه الفترة التى كان مسموح بها زيارة السجين، ماهر كان زميل والدى فى السجن شاب صغير محكوم لمدة سنتين ابتسم لى ولكنى لم اهتم ، بعدما خرج من السجن ذهب الى أمى وسألها الزواج منى وفى هذه الفترة كانت ظروفى صعبة ورأى والدى انه رجل جيد فوافقت على الزواج، أنجبنا ولدين وبنت وبنا لى بيت فى منطقة عناتا قرب العيسوية.

عشنا فترة سعيدة ولكن زوجى مرض وهذا كان فى فترة الحمل بابنى الثالث ورغم مرضه الشديد رفض أن يذهب للعلاج وأصر على البقاء معى لأنى كنت أعانى من الحمل ، بعد فترة أنجبت ابنى وزوجى كان فى حالة ألم شديد وكان لابد أن يذهب الى مستشفى المقاصد القريبة من جبل الزيتون ولأنه يحمل هوية الضفة الغربية واجه صعوبة فى الدخول الى المقاصد فى القدس، وصلنا الى المستشفى وأخبرنا

الطبيب انه وللأسف سيعيش لمدة شهرين لان السرطان انتشر فى كل جسمه واخبره الطبيب بان يذهب ويستمتع فى الوقت المتبقى من حياته.

وفى هذه الفترة كنت ادرس الماجستير وفكرت بأن أؤجل الدراسة، ماهر أصر على أن أكمل الدراسة لان المسؤولية ستكون كبيرة بعد موته، كل يوم كنت أذهب الى المستشفى وأدرس بجانب سرير زوجى، فى هذه الفترة اقترح أخصائى آخر بأنه يمكن معالجة زوجى بالكيماوى فوافقت، وحتى يستمر بالعلاج يجب أن يذهب الى مستشفى إسرائيلى وأخذت الإجراءات وقت طويل وفى اليوم الذى كان مقرر أن يأخذ علاجه توفى.

أود أن أحكى لماذا لا أسكن فى البيت الذى بناه لى ماهر فى قرية عناتا، طبعا نحن نعرف ومنذ بداية بناء الجدار العازل تم فصل عناتا وهى من قرى القدس وسكانها يحملون هوية الضفة الغربية عن العيسوية التى يحمل سكانها الهوية المقدسية، إسرائيل قسمت المناطق الى مناطق أ- ب-ج. وإذا سكنت فى الضفة سأخسر هويتى المقدسية التى حاولت لمدة سبع سنوات أن أحافظ عليها وقد نجحت فى استصدار شهادات ميلاد مقدسية لأبنائى الثلاثة والسبب هو أن الأولاد بالعادة يسجلون فى هوية الأب، والأب يحمل هوية الضفة الغربية وأنا أحمل هوية القدس وهذا يعنى أن الأولاد لا يحملون الهوية نهائيا.

الوضع معقد لنا ولهم ... وهذا وضعنى فى حالة صراع بين أن أذهب وأسكن فى الضفة أو التأمين الصحى لأبنائى بالقدس ... وهذا ما جعلنى أسكن فى بيت صغير مكون من غرفتين نوم، أبنائى فى غرفة وأنا فى غرفة مع كافة أغراضى .

أبنائى دائما يتكلمون عن بيت عناتا بأنه كبير وواسع بأربع غرف ومكان واسع للعب ...

رانية عرفات

Rania and Maher

When my mother and father were in their youth they lived in a village called Aysawiyya. My mother is Buthayna and my father is Moussa. They faced similar problems to Romeo and Juliet but their families only fought for 10 years. My maternal grandparents didn't attend the wedding but my aunt did. When she got home my grandfather beat her and then locked her in her bedroom.

The bigger problem though was that the Israelis arrived at the wedding saying that my father had been involved in a political movement. Involvement in politics is considered to be a crime for Palestinians and is the reason why thirty of my family have been taken prisoner. He was released after two months and my parents subsequently had four daughters and two sons. Later he was arrested for four years, again for political reasons. When he was released they had another three daughters. Then he was arrested again because he actively supported Fatah.

At this time, I was a social worker student at Al Quds University. I used to visit my father every three months which was all that I was allowed. On one visit a young man in the same cell as my father noticed me. He and my father had been in prison together for two years. He smiled at me but I thought nothing of it.

On his release, he came to my mother's house and asked my mother if he could marry me. I was going through a difficult period of my life and my father thought he was a good man so I agreed to marry him. His name was Maher. We had two sons and one daughter and my husband built us a really beautiful home in Anata village, right beside Aysawiyya.

We were very happy until my husband became very ill. This was during my third pregnancy. Although he was in a lot of pain, he didn't want to go to hospital because he thought he should stay with me because I was pregnant. After a few days, my son was born and my husband was in so much pain that he had to go to Al Maqassid Hospital near the Mount of Olives.

We faced many difficulties getting to Jerusalem because my husband has West Bank identity. After we arrived at the hospital, the specialist informed us that he had only two months to live because the cancer had spread through his body. He told us to go and enjoy what little time we had left together.

At this time I was studying for an MA and I wanted to postpone it. Maher said that I must continue because I would have responsibility for our children when he died. So every day I studied in the hospital, sitting beside his bed.

Whilst sitting in the hospital, we met another specialist who thought Maher should have chemotherapy, so I agreed. In order to receive chemotherapy, Maher needed to go to an Israeli hospital, but this took a very long time to arrange. On the very day that he was supposed to begin his treatment, he died.

Now, I would like to tell you about how and why I can't live in the lovely house that Maher built for us. As you will all know, the Israelis began to construct the Wall. It divides Anata from Jerusalem.

People from Anata have West Bank ID and those from Aysawiyya have Israeli ID. The Israelis divided East Jerusalem and the West Bank into Areas A, B and C. This means that if I live in the West Bank, I will lose my East Jerusalem ID which I took seven years to obtain in order get birth certificates for my children. The reason for this is that although we both came from Jerusalem, I had Jerusalem ID but Maher had West Bank ID. This meant that my children had no ID at all.

I know this is very complicated for you; it is also complicated for us. Basically I am faced with the reality that if I go and live in Anata, where the house remains empty, my children and I will lose our Jerusalem identity and, more importantly, we will lose our health insurance. So we live in a very small house, with only two rooms, where all my children share one room.

It would be impossible for me to move and, as you can imagine, my children are always talking about Anata where there are four bedrooms and a garden to play in with a swing.

Rania Arafat

بلا وداع

سيدةٌ بريطانيةٌ تصف موقفاً أثر بها كثيراً خلال لقائها مع النساء الزائرات من فلسطين فى مشروع قصص من أمهاتنا.

روت لى داليةُ الطالبةُ من جامعةُ القدس كيف انه عندما توفى جدها فى القدس لم تتمكن هى او عائلتها من حضور الجنازة.
جدها كان يعيش فى القدس الشرقية المكان الذى لا تستطيع هى وعائلتها الوصول إليه، قالت داليةُ أنها وأمها بكين كثيراً لأنه لم يتسنى لهن إلقاء نظرةُ الوداع على جدها وتوديعه.

لقد تحدثت كثيراً عن هذهُ التجربةُ الأمر الذى أوضح مدى صعوبةُ الحياةُ التى يعيشونها فى فلسطين حيث يحرم الناس من أبسط حقوقهم فى حريةُ التنقل.

ريم [بريطانيا]

96

No goodbye

A British woman describes something that specially affected her when she met the Palestinian women who came to Britain with the Stories from our Mothers project.

I remember Dalia telling me that when her late grandfather passed away, neither she nor any of her family could go over to the funeral as he was in an area of East Jerusalem where they were not allowed.

She speaks of how she and her mother cried so much at not being able to say goodbye to their beloved father/grandfather. She speaks so tenderly of the experience.

It really made it clear how difficult living has become for the Palestinian people that people are denied the most basic of rights which is freedom of movement.

Reem [UK]

قطاف

المسجد الأقصى وهذا أمر مهم جداً بالنسبة لنا فالمسجد الأقصى من أهم مقدساتنا، هو ثالث أهم مسجد للمسلمين فى العالم بعد مسجد مكة والمدينة المنورة فى السعودية، أنها كارثة حقيقية بالنسبة لنا بان نكون مفصولين عن المسجد الأقصى.

لقد قطع الجدار بلدى بيت حنينا الى قسمين ففى سبيل التنقل بين قسمى البلدة الصغيرة عليك ان تتنقل أولا الى رام الله ثم أن تعود الى الطرف الآخر فى رحلة تستغرق فى الباص ساعتين بينما كانت قبل الجدار خمس عشرة دقيقة من المشى.

اذكر عندما كنت طفلة كيف كنت اذهب مع عائلتى كل عام لقطاف الزيتون وكم كنت سعيدة فى رؤية عائلتى تعمل معاً بجد لقطف الثمار كل النساء والأطفال كانوا يساعدوا الرجال فى القطف، كان الرجال يتسلقون الأشجار بينما كانت النساء والأطفال يجمعون الزيتون من الأرض كنت ألهو مع الاطفال بين الأشجار، لا أنسى مذاق طبيخ المقلوبة عندما كنا نتناول الغداء تحت شجر الزيتون.

بعض أشجارنا كانت تبلغ من العمر أكثر من ثلاثمائة سنة كانت كبيرة جداً وكنا نستغرق ثلاث أيام فى قطافها. لم تفارقنى الذكريات الجميلة ولكن قبل ثلاث أيام سألت أبى عن أشجار الزيتون فأجاب بحزن بأنها لم تعد موجودة قال عندما بدأ الإسرائيليون ببناء الجدار قاموا باقتلاعها جميعاً من الوادى لقد اقتلعوا كل أشجار الزيتون التابعة للبلدة.

أنا حزينة جداً أنها خسارة كبيرة للعائلة ولذكرياتى الجميلة ولن أتمكن من مرافقة أولادى لرؤية أشجار الزيتون.

فتحية أبوهلال

أنا طالبة فى السنة الأخيرة فى جامعة القدس المفتوحة متزوجة ولدى خمس أبناء ثلاث بنات وولدين، واعتنى كذلك بوالدا زوجى المسنين ثلاثة من أبنائى يدرسون فى الجامعة وزوجى مهندس زراعى، نقيم فى ابوديس وزوجى يقيم ويعمل فى الولايات المتحدة الأمريكية، مثل العديد من النساء الفلسطينيات واللاتى يعمل أزواجهن فى الخارج اعمل بجد لدى دراستى واطمح بالعمل ما بعد التخرج بالإضافة الى الاعتناء بأولادى.

لدى العديد من النشاطات فانا ازرع الورد واعتنى بها وأحيك المطرزات التراثية الفلسطينية وانا كذلك عضوه فى اللجنة النسويه فى دار الصداقة.

فى الأصل أنا لست من ابوديس لكن من بلدة بيت حنينا وهى داخل نطاق مدينة القدس، يحمل أفراد أسرتى بطاقة الهوية الزرقاء (القدس) فى الوقت الذى انا احمل فيه بطاقة الهوية الخضراء الصادرة من الضفة الغربية، هذا يعنى انه ليس باستطاعتى الذهاب الى القدس بدون الحصول على تصريح مؤقت من قبل السلطات الإسرائيلية وبالعادة لا يصدر هذا التصريح إلا لأسباب صحية علاجية وعليه فانه ليس بإمكانى زيارة أهلى فى القدس بدون الحصول على تصريح بحجة التوجه الى المستشفى، ولأنى مريضة بالسكرى فباستطاعتى أن احصل على تصريح كل ثلاثة أشهر للعلاج وكذلك زيارة أقاربى.

الجدار الإسرائيلى فصلنا عن القدس بطريقه لم نكن لنتخيلها. لازالت أتذكر أيام كنت اذهب مع جدتى لصلاة الجمعة فى

98

Harvest

I am a student in the last year at Al Quds Open University. I have five children, three girls and two boys, and I also look after my elderly mother-in-law and father-in-law. Three of my children are at the university and my husband is a farmer and agricultural expert. He is living in the USA and I stay in Abu Dis with the rest of the family. Like many Palestinian mothers whose husbands work abroad, I work very hard. I have my studies, I will have a job, but I still have my children.

I am a woman of many activities, I like to grow flowers and I make embroidered pictures in the traditional Palestinian style. I am also on the women's committee of Dar Assadaqa.

I'm not from Abu Dis, but from Beit Hanina, a village near Jerusalem. My family have blue Jerusalem ID cards but I have the green ID card issued for the West Bank. This means that I can't go to Jerusalem unless I have a special permit for medical treatment, so I can't visit my family unless I have permission to go to hospital. Because I have diabetes, I can get a permit every three months and then I visit my relatives.

The Wall divides us from Jerusalem in a way I never could have imagined. I remember when I used to go with my grandmother every Friday to pray in the Al Aqsa Mosque. This is very important for us, because Al Aqsa is a very holy place for us. It is the third most important mosque in the world after Mecca and Medina. It is a disaster for us to be divided from Al Aqsa.

The Wall also divides my village, Beit Hanina, into two. To go from one part to the other, you have to go by bus to Ramallah and that takes two hours, where before the Wall was built it took a fifteen minute walk. I can't forget when I was a child, and I went with my family every year to pick the olives and how happy I was to see all the families working hard together. All the wives and children used to help the men. The men climbed the trees and the women picked up the olives from the ground. I used to play in the trees with the other children.

I can't forget how delicious the makloubeh* was when we ate it under the trees. Some of the trees were three hundred years old and they were so big it took three days to pick one.

I can't forget this beautiful memory, but two weeks ago I asked my father when they would start to pick the olives. He answered me sadly saying "There are no olives any more." He said that when they built the Wall, they cut down all the olive trees in the valley, taking them from all the people in the village.

I am very sad. I am shocked. It is a great loss to my family, and I've lost all my beautiful memories. I shall never be able to take my children to see this scene from my childhood.

Fathiyeh Abu Hilal

* Makloubeh – an upside-down dish of rice and chicken, a traditional Palestinian dish

فصل توليد الخراف، روث البقر، ملابس العمل المغطاة بالطين، الفيضانات تصل إلى الباب الخلفي وأقبية اجتاحتها الفيضانات . محصول القمح في المخزن و الشعير فسد في الحقول. الأرانب المسلوخة، الدم الجاري على مصطبة غسل أواني الطبخ. صيادية الكلى وشرائح لحم البقر. البخار المتصاعد من السطول التي تحتوى طعام الخنزير الحار. الأغنام التي تُساق إلى الأسواق على الطرق الريفية ، الرجال الذين يحملون العصي، الأرانب المذبوحة للعشاء، الجراء المحمولة في الحقائب تصارع للخروج قبل أن تلقى مصيرها في نهر سفرن .

وكنت أتخيل أمي تمشي بخفة ورشاقة بين أتلام الشعير الكثيفة واليانعة الخضرة بينما نحدق في الشمس المتوجهة من خلال سعف الشعير الذى يشبه الريش.

أستطيع أن أرى أمي واقفة بمحاذاة البوابة البيضاء المفتوحة بالكاد والمعلقة على مفاصلها في الجزء الأسفل من الحديقة منتظرة مجيئنا من المدرسة . وتحضر القلاية الحديدية الثقيلة وتضعها على الموقد لتقلى البيض ولحم الخنزير المقدد ثم تسكبها على الصحون التي سرعان ما تجد طريقها الى مائدة الأكل الطويلة التي نظفت بعناية.

ويتداخل النهار في المساء . ونأكل وجبة ما قبل العشاء المكونة من الخبز والمربى المطبوخ في البيت والمحفوظ في مرتبانات مصفوفة على رفوف مغطاة بالورق وقد ألصقت عليها بطاقات بيضاء صغيرة تحدد أنواعها: الرازبري، الفراولة، المشمش ، الراوند ، الزنجبيل و التوت ألشوكى بالتأكيد « المربى ب عام 1948». كلها مصنفة بخط أمي الأنيق مرفقة بكلمة «بتاعى» التي ورثتها عنها.

الأم في السروال القصير الأزرق الباهت تشق طريقها بين الشجيرات الشوكية لتلتقط لنا أشهى وأنضر حبات التوت الشوكى لتملأ أفواهنا ولتعبئة سطولنا.

و في الصباح الباكر جدا في العديد من الأيام ، تنادى علينا أمنا بصوت عال «بسرعة، بسرعة « لجمع الفطر. ونركض مشيرات إلى الفطر «هنا، وهنا، وهنا،» حيث القباب المنحنية السلسة المظهر تطل علينا من بين الأعشاب المبللة بالندى.

وفي مرة من المرات، وجدِنا دائرة فطر متكاملة . وقالت الأم «ممنوع اللمس» خوفاً من كسر نفحة السحر واختفاء جميع الفطر من كل الحقول في أنحاء العالم كله.

مارينا 2000

مارينا هي سيدة روسية، كانت طالبة في جامعة موسكو في بداية الثمانينات، حيث التقت جوهر وتزوجته لتذهب معه للعيش في قريته بيت فوريك في فلسطين، لدى مارينا اليوم عائلة مكونه من ولدان وبنت، كما

والدتي مارينا انتقلت بين عالمين روسيا والقواميس العربية المليئة بالجدار.

ولكن بخلاف أمى مارينا واجهت الضغط والانتهاك والاحتلال، لم تتمكن من استقبال رسالة من الوطن الأم روسيا ولم تتمكن من زيارة والديها في روسيا او أن تستقبلهم في فلسطين، ولم يكن بإمكانها المغادرة وإلا فقدت حقها في الرجوع الى فلسطين لم يكن بمقدور أفراد أسرتها الالتقاء مع أهل او العيش معهم.

نحن سعداء جداً بلقائك. لقد اعتقد الناس في القرية أنني أم مرينا التي جاءت لتعيش معها في بيت فوريك عند زيارتي للقرية في المرة الاولى هكذا كان الاعتقاد.

المستوطنون الإسرائيليون استولوا على سفح التلة المطلة على القرية وبدأوا بإطلاق النار في الليل الكل يترقب اقتحام الجنود الإسرائيليون عبر أبواب البيوت.

سفوح التلال تنذر بالقتل والإصابة.

الحواجز والاغلاقات.

اقتحامات من الدبابات الإسرائيلية.

احتلال إسرائيلي، موت فلسطيني، وانتهاكات من قبل المستوطنين.

قصة فريدا أمى وماريا وصديقتي الفلسطينية التقين في ذاكرتي من خلال المشترك بينهما في العيش في عالم آخر عن موطن النشأة طريقة الحياة للعائلة والصراعات التي جمعتهن عبر الزمن كنساء وأمهات.

لقد التقين في ذاكرتي كقطاف التوت الأسود وموسم الزيتون المشى في بيت فوريك والمشى في تلال شروبشر وسياج المزارع وتناول الغداء تحت شجرة زيتون، غرف الماء البارد من الجداول بين يديك، طهى الطعام وعمل المطرزات الجيران والمجتمع.

لقد التقين في الذاكرة في مجتمعين صغيرين عندما تكون العلاقات والرابط الاجتماعية أقوى واقرب حيث يسود جو من التضامن والتآخي بين أفراد المجتمع.

إن مشاركتي في الصراع من أجل تحرير فلسطين من اجل إحلال السلام هي قيمة زرعتها أمي بداخلي خلال السنوات الطويلة الماضية.

لقد سمحت السلطات الإسرائيلية لمارينا بتغيير جواز سفرها وقد تمكنت من زيارات والديها في روسيا بعد سنوات طويلة من الصراع.

بولين كولينز [بريطانيا]

أمهات

كانت أمى فريدةٌ بنت مدينةٍ.

وفى صيف عام 1930 ، ذهبت أمى إلى الريف لنزهةٍ مشى.

وتطلعت أمى من وراء سياج شجيرات الزعرور البرى ورأت رجلا (أبى فيما بعد) يقوم بتمشيط الحقل. وكانت الحقول صغيرةً فى تلك الأيام ، ولم تكن الآلات الصناعيةُ قد وصلت إلى مزارع الريف بعد.

أمى وقعت فى الحب ولكن لم يكن الانسجام كاملا بين المدينة والقرية. وقد استغرق الأمر نزهات مشى عديدةً قبل أن تتمكن الأم التحدث مع الأب. وحُرث الحقل ، و كان أبى يأكل بسكوته تحت شجرة البلوط المحاذية لبوابة المزرعة ذات الخمسة قضبان.

وتأقلمت الأم ، بنت المدينةً ، وهى الآن زوجةُ فلاح ، على العيش فى بيت المزرعة الرطب والبارد الواقع على منعطف مجرى نهر سفرن.

وفى الصباح قبل طلوع الفجر ، نوافذ البيت مطليةٌ بالصقيع الأبيض. تندفع أمى إلى المطبخ وتشعل الضوء وهى ترتعش من البرد وتحضر طعام الإفطار لعمال المزرعة الذين كانوا قد بدأوا عملهم اليومى.

وفى وقت لاحق ، تمشى الأم على طريق ملتو يقود إلى مبانى المزرعة حاملةً طعام الدجاج

والخنازير . وكان الديك بالانتظار ومنقاره جاهز لينقر الحافة العليا لجزمتها وبسرعةٍ ينقرها للمرة الثانية زاعقا بصوت حاد و مغرور قبل أن تتمكن الأم من الهرب والسطل يتأرجح فى يدها لتطعم الخنازير. وظلت علامات النقر هذه على أرجل الأم باديةً للعيان لسن متأخرة . عاشت القرية والمدينة معا ولكن لم تكن العيشة سهلة.

أشياء من المدينة ، أصدقاء، طقوم الشاى ، محادثات واهتمامات . أفلام سينمائية: الأم العجوز رايلى ، جورج فورمبى وجون وبين فى «النهر الأحمر». الاستماع بالسمك والبطاطا المقلية من المدينة وشراء الكعك من الدكاكين.

101

Mothers

FREIDA 1930

Freida, my mother, was a town girl.

Mother took a walk in the country in the summer of 1930. Mother looked over a hawthorn hedge and father was harrowing a field. Fields were small in those days. Industry had not come to the country farm.

Mother fell in love. An uneasy match between town and country.

It took many walks, before mother spoke to father. The field ploughed. My father eating his snap under the oak tree by the five-barred gate.

Mother, a town girl, now a farmer's wife, learnt to live in the damp, draughty farmhouse within the turn of the river Severn.

Mornings, before it was light, the windows white with frost, started with a dash to the kitchen, lighting the kitchen range and shivering, laying breakfast out for farm workers already well into their day's labour.

Later, walking down the twisting path to the farm buildings, with chicken feed and pig swill, the cockerel waited. Beak ready to peck above her wellington boots and quickly get her again with a self satisfied squawk as she ran, pail slopping, to feed the pigs. Red pecked legs years later told the tale. Town and country mixed with difficulty in our lives.

Towny objects, friends, tea sets, talk, interests. Cinema , Old Mother Riley, George Formby, John Wayne in "Red River". Treats of towny fish and chips and bought cake.

Lambing, cow muck, work clothes covered with mud, floods up to the back door and flooded cellars. Harvest home and barley rotted in the fields.

Skinned rabbits, blood running across the scullery floor, steak and kidney pudding boiling in the copper over the week's washing. Hot pig swill steaming in buckets, sheep walked to market along country roads, men with sticks, rabbits killed for supper, puppies in bags struggling before meeting the water of the Severn.

In my mind's eye I can see mother walking in the green density of barley rows getting lighter and lighter as we squinted at the sun glowing through the feathery fronds.

I can see Mother standing by the white gate, propped open, hanging off its hinges at the bottom of our garden, waiting for us to come home from school. Taking down the big iron frying pan, putting it on the stove, tipping bacon and eggs into plates on the long scrubbed kitchen table.

Days slid into evenings. There were scones for tea, homemade jam from jars lined up on paper lined shelves. The names written on small white labels. Raspberry, strawberry, gooseberry, rhubarb and ginger, blackberry: definitely blackberry. "My jam, 1948". All labelled in Mother's neat writing with the 'm' that I have inherited.

Mother in faded blue shorts pushing between prickly bushes finding the most succulent berries to stuff in our mouths and fill pails.

Early, early many mornings mother would shout "hurry, hurry" for mushroom picking. We ran, pointing "here, here, here, here," as smooth curved domes peeped up through the dew covered grass.

Once, a perfect round mushroom circle. Mother said "don't touch" for fear of breaking the magic spell and all the mushrooms in all the fields in all the world would vanish.

MARINA 2000

Marina was a Russian girl.
Marina was at Moscow University in the early eighties.
Marina met Yoher.
Marina married Yoher and went to live in Beit Fourik, Palestine.

Marina had a family, two sons and a daughter.

Like Mother, Marina adjusted to two worlds. Russian words, Arabic dictionaries. Kandinsky on the wall.

Unlike Mother, Marina faces:
Oppression – violence – occupation.
No letters from her Russian home.
No visits to mum and dad.
No visits from mum and dad.
No permission to come home to Palestine if she leaves.
No family life with grandparents.

"We are so pleased to see you. Marina, your mother has come to be with you at last," repeated over over again, my identity mistaken as I become, to the villagers, Marina's long awaited mother.

Israeli settlers stalking down over the hill.
Gun shots.
Nights waiting for soldiers to break through the door.

Hillsides of olives and figs unharvested for seven years.
Hillsides of death and injury

Checkpoint closures. Israeli tank incursions.

Israeli occupation – Palestinian death – settler violence.

Freida and Marina, my Mother and my Palestinian friend meet in my memory of country ways, family ways and struggles they share over time as women and mothers.

They meet in my memories of blackberry picking, olive harvest, walking in the Beit Fourik and Shropshire hills, ploughing the fields, eating lunch under the olive trees, cupping the cool water from the spring in our hands, cooking and sewing, neighbours and community.

They meet in the memories of small community life when we lived closely with one another and depended on each other.

In the shared struggle to free Palestine through the values of peace and justice passed on to me from my mother all those years ago.

Pauline Collins [UK]

Marina has now got her passport changed by the Israeli authorities and has visited her mother and father in Russia after many years of struggle.

103

غــزة 9-2008

Gaza 2008-9

يوم يهاجمونا ويطلقون القنابل ليست صوت وإنما قنابل حقيقية. حتى الجامعة التي كنت ادرس فيها تم قصفها بالقنابل وكان صعب على الذهاب الى الجامعة واستكمال دراستها.

عام 2008 أصبح الحصار اشد لا يوجد كهرباء كانت منطقتنا تحصل على الكهرباء لمدة ثمان ساعات يومياً، وهذا أفضل من مناطق أخرى على اعتبار أن الكهرباء كانت تتوفر مرة كل ثلاث او اربع أيام فى العديد من المناطق، لا يوجد وقود للسيارات ولا يوجد أدوية.

كان لأختى ولدان صغار فكانت تبحث فى كل غزة من اجل الحصول على دواء وفوط لأولادها وكل المواصلات توقفت المواصلات العامة كما السيارات الخاصة توقفت لأنه لا يوجد وقود.

إحدى الاختراعات الفلسطينية هى أن أصبح الناس يستخدمون زيت الخضار كبديل للوقود، حيث أصبحت تمشى فى الشارع وتشتم رائحة المقلى ليس لديهم أى خيار، أبى مصاب بالضغط والإمراض مثل السكرى والضغط لا يوجد لها أدوية والمرضى يجب أن يأخذوا الدواء باستمرار.

هذه الحياة اليومية ولم أتكلم عن تفاصيل أناس مثل أناس أرادوا السفر من أجل العلاج التعليم، فهناك حصار على الناس من كل الاتجاهات والذى يستطيعون الخروج هى الحالات المرضية الخطيرة جدا وفى حالة وفاة ...هؤلاء فقط قادرون على مغادرة غزة والكثير منهم مات قبل أن يحصل على تصريح...

أنا محظوظة لأننى حصلت على فرصة للدراسة فى لندن وأنا الآن خارج غزة أريد أن احكى لكم عن نضالى للخروج من غزة ... حصلت على تصريح للخروج بمساعدة السفارة البريطانية فى القدس، قال الإسرائيليون اذا خرجتى لن تستطيعين العودة مرة أخرى، وهذا ما يقولون للجميع ولكن الفلسطينيون يخرجون ويرجعون مرة أخرى.

كنت بلندن حين وقعت الحرب ضد غزة وعائلتى تسكن قرب مجلس الوزراء بغزة ـ مجمع الوزارات واحد الأبنية هناك ضربت بصاروخ من طائرة اف 16 ، وكان الصوت ضخم جدا وضرب على المبنى 16 صاروخ فإذا كان صاروخ واحد مدمر فما بالكم بهذا العدد ، حاولت أن اتصل مع أهلى ولكن لم استطع واعتقدت أنهم ماتوا ولم أستطع أن أصل لهم وأصبحت ابحث عنهم فى قوائم الأموات، بعد يومين استطاعت أن اتصل بأمى التى كانت عائدة لبيت أخيها، حيث أن بيتنا تدمر وعائلتى نجت وكان بين كل صاروخ وآخر 5 دقائق حيث هربت أمى فى هذه

حياة أمى تأثرت بشكل كبير بالحربين العالميتين الأولى والثانية، ولدت أمى فى العام 1920 ثمانى عشر شهراً بعد انتهاء الحرب العالمية الأولى فى العام 1918، لم تعرف والدها لان والداها انفصلا قبل ولادتها...

ولدت أنا فى لندن بعد ساعتين من انطلاق صفارات الإنذار للتحذير من غارة جوية فى العام 1943 خلال الحرب العالمية الثانية، أخبرتنى والدتى بعد سنوات أن إدارة المستشفى كانت تخرج الأطفال حديثى الولادة الى الممرات فى المستشفى خارج غرفهم لحمايتهم من القصف.

كلا والداى وجدى وجدتى تجنبوا كل الوقت الحديث عن الحروب، ما خلفته الحرب من فقدان للعلاقات بين الناس والألم كان كبير جداً لدرجة أنهم فضلوا عدم الحديث عنها.

لورنا آركشر

106

الفترة، وكان أبى وأمى فى البيت وكانوا يخفون أولادهم فى أجسادهم ليحموه من الإصابة فقدوا بيتهم ولكنهم نجوا.

لدى قصة أخرى، تدمير المنزل أصبح أهلى يبحثون عن تعويض، ولكن الاونروا تريد أن تعوض فقط اللاجئين والسكان الباقون يأخذون من undp ولكن لم يعطوهم لان أمى كانت لاجئة وأرسلوها للاونروا من جديد، وهكذا بين المؤسستين ضاع حق أهلى بين لاجئين وغير لاجئين ولا زالوا الى اليوم.

حاولت الذهاب الى غزة واستطاعت الذهاب من خلال مصر وانتظرت ثلاث أيام وكنت محظوظة لأن هناك من ينتظر أشهر .... وقصتى أحسن من قصص أخرى.

إيناس البيطار [بريطانيا]

عائلتي في غزة

أريد أن أحدثكم عن عائلتي في غزة وهي أيضا قصة عامة حدثت مع الكثيرين في غزة، قصتي أنني حين أنهيت المدرسة وودت الذهاب الى الجامعة حيث كنت أود أن ادرس في جامعة بير زيت، تقدمت بطلب وقبلت في الجامعة لكن المشكلة كانت كيف سأذهب الى هناك.

بير زيت في الضفة الغربية وأنا في غزة قدمت تصريح للذهاب الى الضفة فحصلت على تصريح لمدة يومين فقط، واكتشفت أن هذا ليس لي فقط وإنما لكل الطلاب الذين يريدون الدراسة في الضفة، يحصلون على تصريح لمدة يومين فقط.

لدى صديقة حصلت على تصريح لمدة يومين وبقيت هناك دون أن تعود أمي وأبي رفضوا الفكرة على اعتبار أنني سأخسر إمكانية العودة أبدا الى غزة.

بقيت في غزة ودرست هناك وأصبحت الحياة أسوء فأسوء حتى عام 2006 حيث بدأت قصة الحصار على غزة.

أصبحت الحياة أسوء يوم بعد يوم ، في غزة لا يوجد جيش إسرائيلي ولكنهم يحاصرون الحدود وطائراتهم في السماء، وكل

My family in Gaza

I'm going to talk about my story in Gaza; it represents everybody's story in Gaza.

I am going to start my story from when I finished school and wanted to go to university. I wanted to study at Bir Zeit in the West Bank. I applied and got accepted.

The problem was how to get to Bir Zeit - how to go to the West Bank. We went through the normal way of applying to get a permit. They gave me a permit for two days only. I discovered that this is not only my story but this is the same story for everyone; when students in Gaza want to go to West Bank to study, they are given permits for only 2 days. I have friends that got the permit for two days, and went to the West Bank for two days for university. But for me, my parents said no.

So I stayed in Gaza and I started my university in Gaza. Then, life got much worse, especially, from 2006 when the siege started.

Life was getting more difficult day by day. We don't have Israeli soldiers on the ground like you have in the West Bank but we have an army in the sky and in planes. There was bombing every day and, when I say every day, I mean every day. It wasn't just sound bombs but real bombs too. The university I was studying at was bombed which made it difficult for me to go to university and to continue my education.

By 2008, the siege became much worse so there was no electricity. We used to have electricity in my area only 8 hours a day. This was considered to be good; some areas used to have electricity only once every 3 or 4 days.

There was no fuel for cars. There was no medicine and my sister has two kids. She used to go through the whole of the Gaza strip to get milk and medicine for the children. The transport system completely stopped, including personal cars, and we stayed that way for a few months.

We came up with the idea of using vegetable oil and mixing it up with other things to use as petrol in the cars. Actually, you walk in the street and it smells like fries are being cooked! But that was it, we didn't have any other choice.

My father has high blood pressure and the medicine for such diseases, and diabetes, is not sufficient.

This is daily life and not to mention what happens if someone is sick/works/studies and wants to travel. Of course the blockade for people is complete; no one can travel or get in or out. Getting out of Gaza is only for special cases, for example when someone is very, very sick – when I say very sick, I mean when they are about to die. Those are the only people that manage to leave Gaza at this time.

Many people die before they get the permits, whether it's through Israel or through Egypt.

I got the chance to study in London and the question was how I was going to get out of Gaza. I want to talk a little bit about this now. When I applied, in September 2008, it was much easier than it is now because I got the support of the British Embassy in Jerusalem and they helped me to get out. But the Israelis said, "Once you get out, that's it, you're not coming back again". Of course, they say this to everyone but we try and go anyway.

I was in London when the war in Gaza happened [2008-9] and I am going to tell my family's story. We lived next to a ministry compound and they bombed one of these ministers with a rocket from an F16. The sound was so huge that you couldn't really even hear it.

I read in the news that they bombed this compound with sixteen of these rockets from F16s. I was trying to reach my family for two days and I couldn't reach them; I thought they had died.

I searched for their names in the lists of the people that had died. I was searching for their names because I couldn't get hold of them and all those rockets had been fired. After 2 days, I managed to reach my mother; they had escaped to my uncle's house. Our house had been completely demolished but my family survived. My mother told me that there had been a five-minute break between the first ten rockets and the second ten rockets. There were twenty rockets. They managed to run away in

> **Two World Wars had a very significant influence on my mother's life. She was born in 1920, eighteen months after the end of World War 1, in 1918, and never knew her father because her parents had parted before she was born...**
>
> **Only hours after an air raid warning in 1943, I was born in London during World War 2. My mother told me many years later that the new-born babies were wheeled out into the hospital corridor until it was safe...**
>
> **Both my parents and my grandparents were very reluctant to talk about the wars. The loss of relationships and the pain associated with this was probably too much to bear.**
>
> **Lorna Archer [UK]**

Now I am going to continue by discussing refugees because my mother is a refugee but my father is not. Now the war has ended, we need to talk about compensation. They were saying that UNRWA was going to compensate the refugees and that the non-refugees would be compensated by UNDP.

So, we went to UNDP because the house is in the name of my father who is not a refugee. When we got there they said no because my mother is a refugee; they told us to go to UNRWA. So, we went to UNRWA and they said no because the house was not registered in my mother's name; they told us to go to UNDP. So we have not been compensated, but we are still working on it.

I was determined to go back to Gaza last summer and I managed to get back and it took me three days to cross the border from Egypt. I was lucky because some people wait for months but I only had to wait for 3 days.

these five minutes, my parents and my brother. My mother told me that they were covering my brother with their bodies. Thank God they all survived, but we did lose our house.

And that is my story. But I am telling you that my story is much better than other people's stories.

Enass Albittar

109

جنتي المفقودة

قصيدة مهداه الى الأمهات المناضلات فى فلسطينى

قالت انه من الأفضل البقاء فى الداخل
وهى تشد على يدى بقوة
تحاول استسماح رصاصات الحب التى سرقتها منى.

فى أنفاسها العزيزة الأخيرة
غنت لى أغنيت ما قبل النوم من الزمن البعيد، عن أرض
وعدت بان تكون لى
ابتسمت تلك الابتسامة العريضة كعيد قمرى
وهمست بنعومة
تحلى بالشجاعة طفلى

فالله سيكون دوما الى جانبك
بعد اربع أيام طويلة، وأربع ليالى طويلة جاؤا وقالوا لماذا لم أغادر
قلت لهم لان الجنة تحت أقدام الأمهات.

شعر لشيميزا رشيد

من بريطانيا [بريطانيا]

110

My lost heaven

A poem dedicated to the
brave Mothers of Palestine

She said it was better to stay inside,
as she held my hands tight,
trying to forgive the bullets of love she stole
from me.

And with her precious last breaths,
she sang me the lullaby of a distant time,
of a land she promised would be mine.
She smiled that beaming smile like the
glorious Eid moon
and softly whispered
My child, be brave,
as Allah will always be by your side.

After four long days and four lonely nights,
they came and asked
Why did I not leave?
I told them it was because (Janath) 'heaven'
lay at my mother's feet.

Shemiza Rashid [UK]

111

التمييز في كـل
مناحي حياتنا

Discrimination in
every part of our lives

طفولة

هناك حوالى خمس عائلات فلسطينيةٍ تعيش حول مستوطنى تل رميده، وعليه فنحن الأقرب الى المستوطنة.

فى الأصل هى أرضنا لكن الإسرائيليون استولوا عليها كما استولوا على أراضى أخرى من ملاكها العرب، لقد أخذوا الأرض بالقوة ويعش المستوطنين بها الآن بدل منا، توجد الآن نقطةٌ عسكريةٌ إسرائيليةٌ بالقرب منا.

لدى أربع أبناء وبنت، أحد أبنائى وبنتى أكثرنا معاناةً منى ومن باقى الأسرة لما حدث لهم على أيدى المستوطنين.

كل يوم يتعرض أبنائى للتفتيش من قبل الجنود يتم تفتيش محتويات حقائبهم المدرسية، كما لو أنهم يقطعون معبر دولى، فى الوقت الذى يحصل أبناء المستوطنين على كل شىء، يحرم أبناءنا من أبسط الأشياء، ابتداء من حصولهم على أماكن للعب حتى خروجهم وعودتهم الى البيت.

لدينا أرضنا ولكن لا يحق لنا اللعب فيها، ولا حتى كرةُ القدم، ويدفع المستوطنين بأولادهم الى أرضنا ليلعبوا ويستمعوا بوقتهم ولا أحد يستطيع إيقافهم.

لا يستطيع الصغار تحمل ما يحدث، حتى وإن تحمله الكبار، لأن صغارنا يقارنون حياتهم بحياةً أبناء المستوطنين، (لماذا يسمح لهم التحرك كما يحلو لهم بينما نمنع نحن).

أطفالنا فى خطر كل الوقت يتعرضون للضرب خاصةً أيام السبت.

هذا ابنى، اسمه أحمد وهو فى العاشرة من العمر، كان فى طريق عودته من المدرسة وبيده كرةُ قدم يلعب بها فى أرضنا، لم يلاحظ وجود المستوطنين خلفه، نحن على الدوام حذرون من المستوطنين ولكن لم ينتبه هو.

أمسك به عدد من المستوطنين كانوا أكبر منه سناً، كانوا شباب تتراوح أعمارهم بين 18 وعشرون عاماً، ضربوه بحجر على عينه وألقوا الحجارة على رأسه، أرضنا تقع على منحدر بحيث هناك مستويان للأرض حمل المستوطنين طفلى وألقوا به من مكان مرتفع، وقد أغمى عليه على الفور نتيجةً لذلك.

لم نكن لنعلم ما حدث له لولا جيران لنا قاموا بالاتصال بنا وأخبرونا أن طفلنا يتعرض للقتل، خرجت أنا ووالده وابنتى هيا، رفض المستوطنون أن يعطونا أحمد أرادوا أن يستمروا فى ضربه.

لم نكن نعرف ما يمكن فعله، ماذا سيكون شعورك لو

سيدةٌ بريطانية تصف موقفاً خاصاً أثر فيها خلال زيارتها لفلسطين فى مشروع قصص من أمهاتنا.

قابلت سيدة فلسطينية حكت لى قصة أختها التى تعيش فى مخيم للاجئين مع ابنتها .... تعانى بنت أختها من صدمةٍ نفسية شديدة، أدت الى فقدانها السيطرة على نفسها فهى تبلل فراشها وملابسها بدون سيطرة، وهى تتلقى علاج خاص.

كان ذلك نتيجة تجربه صعبه مرت بها عندما شاهدت معلمها يقتل أمام أعينها فى المدرسة.

شاهدتى طفلك يتعرض لهذه المعاملة، لذلك فقد قمنا بالاشتباك مع المستوطنين. لقد مكنت اشتباكنا مع المستوطنين والد الطفل من أن ينزل الى حيث وقع أحمد وأن يلتقطه، لم يكن لدينا سيارةٌ وكان يتوجب علينا أن نحمل أحد من خس عشرةً الى عشرون دقيقة مشياً على الأقدام حتى نصل الى الشارع العام، لا يوجد مواصلات عامة فى منطقتنا إلا للمستوطنين، وصل ابنى السيارة وحالته يرثى لها، كان مغمى عليه وقد نزف كميةً كبيرةً من الدم.

عند وصولنا الى الحاجز العسكرى، أوقفنا الجنود، وسألنا عن ما حدث، قبل أن نتابع طريقنا الى المستشفى، هذا صورة ابنى التقطت عند وصولنا الى المستشفى ونشرت فى صحيفة محلية، بقى ابنى فاقداً للوعى لمدة ثلاث أيام.

كل يوم سبت نتعرض للهجوم من قبل المستوطنين، لدينا خياران إما أن نبقى حبيسى بيوتنا أو أن نتعرض للرشق بالحجارة.

حمداً لله فهو لازال مواظب على دراسته، لكنه لازال يعانى من مشاكل نفسية نتيجة لما حدث.

سهى الحداد

Childhood

There are about five families living around the settlement of Tel Rumeida so we are the closest ones to that settlement.

Originally, it was our land but the Israelis took it and they took the land of other Arab people and lived in their place. They took the land from its owners by force and the settlers lived there instead, and now there is a big military unit near us.

I have four sons and three daughters. My sons and daughters suffer the most from the settlers, more than me and more than their father.

Every day, my children have to show the soldiers the contents of their bags and have a body search, as if they are at an international frontier. The settlers'

children have everything, whereas our children are deprived of everything – everything from games to coming and going.

We have land which we are not allowed to play on – not even football. The settlers however put their children onto our land where they play and enjoy their time and no one says anything about it.

The children can't tolerate this, even if the older people can. This is because they compare themselves to the settlers' children – "Why are they allowed to do whatever they want whilst we are not?"

Our children are at risk of being beaten daily, especially on the Sabbath.

This is my son, his name is Ahmad and he is 10 years old. He was returning from

116

Settlers in the old city of Hebron, guarded by the Israeli army

مستوطنين في البلدة القديمة في الخليل محاطون بحراسة من الجيش الإسرائيلي

school with a football which he had brought from school and he was playing with it on our private land. He did not see the settlers behind him. We are careful of the settlers but he was not.

The settlers grabbed him and they were older boys, who were between 18 and 20 years old, not young I mean. They threw rocks at his eyes, first of all, and then they threw rocks at his head and then grabbed him. At our home, we have some land on two levels – an upper level and a lower level. They carried him and then threw him from the higher ground onto the lower ground; he fell unconscious.

We would not have seen him at all if it not been for the neighbours who called us on the phone and told us that our son was about to be killed. So his father and I went outside with my daughter, Haya, but the settlers refused to give him to us; they wanted to continue beating him.

We didn't know what we could do – what do you feel when you see your son being treated like that? So we started to fight and the settlers fought too. The dispute gave his father the chance to go down and get his son from the lower land. We don't have a car so you have to walk for fifteen to twenty minutes until you reach the main road; there is no transport in our area except for the settlers. So my son did not reach a car until he was in a very bad way; he was unconscious and losing blood.

When we got to the checkpoint in the main road, they stopped us. They asked what was going on and what was happening. After the checkpoint, we took him in the car to the hospital. This is a picture from the news of his condition when we reached the hospital. He stayed unconscious for three days.

There was no particular reason for this. Every Saturday we get attacked. We have two choices – either stay in the house or get hit by stones. Thank God, my son regularly attends school again. But he still suffers the psychological effects, even now.

Suha Alhadad

معاناة طفلة فلسطينية

ماذا عساى أن أكتب
وقلمى ملكةُ الأفعال والأمور
ودفترى بالمتفجرات ملغوم
وفى قلبى جرح لا يزول ولا يموت
والدنيا أثقلتها الهموم

ماذا أفعل فى مكان وعالم..
يدور ولن يدوم وكيف أتجاهل نداء أقصى يغرق بدماء أم صرخةَ مظلوم
ماذا عساى أن أنتظر الصدف أم الجرح لكى يزول ألأتكلم ؟؟

وقلمى قد ضاع وسط الحقول ماذا أقول ؟
والعدو قد أدمن على شرب دمائنا كالكحول ونحن تحت القصف منذ قرون

ماذا عساى أن أقول والعصافير من بيوتها ها هى تؤول وشفتاى قد أصابهما الذبول مَنْ ألـــوم ؟؟ شعبى .أم قدرنا المزعوم وكيف أدافع ؟؟

وانا لا أملك سوى الحجر لأ دافع بماذا عساى أن أضحى وأرضى قد أحيطت بجدار الفصل وكيف أقبل الذل ؟؟

وأنا لغيرك يا ربى لست براكع وانا طفلةً لا أقوى على صد المدافع إذا ما ناديت من عساه سيسمع صوتى الباكى ولماذا أنتظر ؟؟

وشعبى هنا ما زال يُحْتَضَر بماذا عساى أن أنهى كلماتى وأنا طفلةً وهذه حقيقةُ معاناتى

داليةُ أبوهلال
طالبةٌ فى جامعةُ القدس أبوديس

Poem for Palestinian children

The poet is a student at the Al Quds University in Abu Dis. She explains about her poem:

It is about the emotional suffering of a Palestinian girl who thinks she has nothing to protect herself with except a handful of stones. She then says that maybe it is better to write about her suffering and her feelings about not being able to see Jerusalem and Al Aqsa, she cannot ignore these feelings.

"What can I do for my country that is now encircled by this ugly wall?

"How can I accept the cruel glances of the soldiers when I feel humiliated and have a duty only to God, not to them?"

I hope you understand what I am trying to explain.

Dalia Abu Hilal

تخرجت من جامعة القدس مع درجة مميزة فى العام الماضى فى طب الاسنان، أعيش مع عائلتى فى ابوديس منذ العام 2005 وأود أن احكى لكم قصة والدتى.

لقد كان ذلك قبل 27 عام حين هاجر عمى من بيته فى فلسطين، حيث عاشت عائلتى ظروفا سيئة نصف العائلة كان يعيش فى مخيمات فى الأردن وقد استولى الإسرائيليون على أرضنا بعد الاحتلال عام 67. اعتمدت عائلتى على الزراعة، مزرعتهم وأشجار الزيتون والقمح الذى كان كنز جدتى الثمين، وقد سرقت الأرض.

كان زفاف عمى مناسبة جيدة للقاء العائلة وبعد أسبوع من زواجه غادر عمى الأردن الى الكويت وعمل هناك فى شركة بترول، آخر مكالمة منه كانت قبل أكثر من شهر، ولم يسمع احد منه بعد ذلك، لم يعرف احد أين هو.

حاولت عائلتى جاهدة لمعرفة أين يمكن أن يكون ولكن دون جدوى، ولا زالت جدتى تنتظر، لا تزال زوجته بالانتظار فهى إنسانه مؤمنه ولا تعرف اليأس. لقد انتظرت وحيدة فى الأردن، أنا أتأمل أن يعود وان أراه مرة أخرى لم اعرفه ولكن اعلم بأنه كان رجلا صالحا.

جدتى كانت تبلغ الخمسين من العمر عندما قتل جدى دهسا تحت عجلات حافلة إسرائيلية فى طريق عودته من العمل تاركا وراءه أرمله وستة بنات، لم يكن هناك من يساعدها على العيش.

لذلك قررت بان تزوج بناتها لأول من يدق بابها، كان هذة خيارها لا اعرف اذا كان صواب ام خطأ ولكن لو كنت مكانها

ما فعلت. لازالت جدتى على قيد الحياة وتذكر كل تفاصيل حياتها، الفقر والحياة الصعبة والاحتلال البغيض كل هذة الظروف جعلتها تطوى أجنحتها على صغارها.

استطيع أن أقول أننا ورثنا عنها الكثير من قوتها وشجاعتها، أنا واثنتين من شقيقاتى تعلمنا فى الجامعة رغم قساوة ظروفا، يعمل والدى فى البناء فى المستوطنات الإسرائيلية، كنصف العمل الفلسطينيين، ونعلم أن العمل توقف بعد بناء الجدار الفاصل، وعليه فقد تأثر وضعنا المادى وعلى الرغم من قساوة الظروف لدينا ثقة بالله وانه سيساعدنا.

أختى فى السنه الخامسة فى كلية الطب والثانية فى كلية الصيدلة، تعمل أمى بالخياطة وقد أنجزت الكثير من العمل من اجل أن تشترى لنا كتب وملابس.

عمل الفقر دورا هاما فى حياتنا وقد غير اتجاه حياتنا كلياً لكن من يعتقد فى العمل والجهد يحصلون على ما يريدون. أملى بان أكمل دراستى وسأفعل ذلك أن لم يكن الآن فسيكون فى القادم من حياتى.

اعذرونى اذا كان هناك أخطاء فى اللغة فهذه المرة الأولى التى اكتب فيها ما يجول بخاطرى، انه إحساس جيد، شكراً على إتاحة هذة الفرصة لى للمشاركة فى ما أفكر فيه مع الناس فى بريطانيا، لقد سعدت بلقاء من زارونا فى مناسبتين أو ثلاثة، أمل بان تمكنا هذة العلاقة من إيصال صوتنا بطريقة أفضل للعام.

شيماء أبو فارة

Studying

I graduated from Al Quds University last year with a very good degree as a general dentist. I have been living with my family in Abu Dis since 2005. I want to share with you in telling our mother's stories.

Twenty-seven years ago, my uncle left his home in Palestine. At that time my family lived in very bad circumstances: half of the family had moved to the camps in Jordan and big parts of their land had been stolen after the Israeli Occupation. They had been dependent on agriculture. The farm, olive trees and wheat were my grandmother's treasure. But they were gone.

My uncle's marriage was a chance to see all the family. After one week he moved to Jordan then to Kuwait. He found a job there with an oil company. The last call from him was after one month. After that no one heard from him or saw him. Nobody knows where he was.

My family tried hard to find where he was, but it was hopeless. My grandmother is still waiting. His wife is the most faithful women I have ever seen in my life: she never gives up. She is waiting, lonely, in Amman. I hope he will return and see how much we love him. I do not know him but I can tell that he was a good man.

The next year, my grandmother was fifty years old; she was again facing her destiny. Her husband died, he was crushed by an Israeli bus when he was on his way back home. The darkness of the life increases with time. Who could help this old widow? No one.

The only solution she found was to marry her six daughters to the first men who knocked at her door. That was her choice. Is it right or wrong I don't know, but if I were her I would never do that.

My grandmother is still alive and remembers every minute in her life. The poverty, the difficult life, the ugly Occupation that forced her to keep her children under her wings.

I can say at this moment that we inherited some of her strength. I and my two sisters study in the university even though it is a very difficult life. My father worked as a builder in the Israeli settlements, just like half of the Palestinian people. And you know that this work was stopped by the Separation Wall. So our financial resources are often very limited – even though we have a passion to study and our God helps us all of the time.

My middle sister is in the fifth year of medicine and the second one in the pharmacy faculty. My mother does sewing work, she does a lot of work and helps in buying our books, our clothes.

Poverty has played a part in our life, the Occupation has changed the destiny of our life, but people who have belief in their heart work hard to get what they want.

My passion is to complete my study in the oncology department. I will do it, if not now it will be at the end of my life.

Forgive me if make any mistake in spelling or words, this the first time I write what is going in my heart. It is a very nice feeling.

Thank you for giving us the chance to share our ideas with the British people, I enjoyed meeting them. I hope that this gives us a chance to introduce ourselves better to the world.

Shaima Abu Farah

البيت

حسناً نحن الآن فى منطقة القدس الشرقية فى منطقة فلسطينية، هناك
28 عائلة فلسطينية تعيش فى هذة المنطقة، الرجل الواقف بالقميص
المبلط هناك، تم إخلاءه من منزله اعتقد بان المنزل يخصه، عائلة
إسرائيلية عائلة مستوطنين انتقلت للعيش فى المنزل.

فيما يظهر أفراد العائلة الفلسطينية وهم حرفياً يعيشون على الشارع
بعد أن طردوا من بيتهم.

كذلك الجيران يتواجدوا فى المكان وهم أيضا قلقون للغاية،
فهى بالنسبة لهم مسألة وقت وسيتم إخراجهم من منزلهم، هم
يخوضون الآن معركة طويلة فى المحاكم الإسرائيلية من اجل
استعادة منزلهم ولكن حتى محاميهم وعلى الرغم من انه قدم كل
الدلائل على ملكيتهم للمنزل لازالوا يعيشون فى الشارع.

هذا حقيقة ما يحدث هنا.

أنيسة

سيدة أخرى كانت موجودة تصف ما كان يحدث فى الثانى من آب
طردت عائلة الغاوى من منزلهم الذى موجود خلفى وهم الآن ينامون
فى الشارع، كل العائلة تنام فى الشارع وجاءت العديد من المجموعات
الدولية للبقاء والتضامن معهم ودعمهم على أمل مساعدتهم فى
معركتهم ضد السيطرة على القدس الشرقية والضم الغير شرعى
للقدس الشرقية

Home

Okay, we're just on the suburbs of Jerusalem, we've just come here in a Palestinian area. There's twenty-eight families, twenty-eight Palestinian families that were living in this area, and the gentleman over there in the checkered shirt, he's just been evicted, and I think that was his home there, so a Jewish settlement, a Jewish family, an Israeli family has just sort of come in.

These are the other members of the family out here and they're literally living on the road.

His neighbours are around here as well, and the neighbours are saying it's literally only a matter of time now, and they're going to be evicted. They were put through a really long court battle and even though his lawyer put through all the right documents for him, they're still being thrown out, so that's what's happening.

Anisah [UK]

Another woman met at the scene described what was happening:

On the 2nd of August, the Al-Ghawi family was evicted from their home just behind me, and they've been sleeping on the street ever since. The entire family has been sleeping on the street as a sign of protest, and many international groups have come to stay with them as a sign of solidarity with them to support them in their cause, and hopefully aid them in their fight against the takeover of East Jerusalem, the illegal annexation of East Jerusalem.

123

كان زوجى وابنى يقفان بالقرب من خيمة الذل والهوان ..
عندما بدأت أصرخ فى وجه الجنود بأن لا يقتربوا من أى
واحدة منا.. كان الرد من الجندى سريعاً ومباغتاً أن لا خروج
لكم اليوم عن البوابة.. بعد أن هدّدوا زوجى بالضرب والاعتقال
إن لم نعد من حيث أتينا... عدنا والعود غير أحمد فى هذه
المرة .. عدنا وعروقنا تغلى فيها الدماء.. قهراً وإيلاماً.. فلا
يوجد منفذ واحد للخروج

بكت ابنتى لحرمانها من حقها الطبيعى فى الذهاب إلى
مدرستها .. وساد الوجوم وجوهنا لا ندرى ما نحن فاعلون... لم
أعد إلى البيت مباشرة ، فضّلت أن أعرّج على مدرسة القرية
.. حيث أمارس عملى فى الإشراف.

ما زال بعض طلبة المدرسة حتى اللحظة فى ساحة
المدرسة ينتظرون معلميهم ومعلماتهم والذين هم على
الجانب الآخر من الجدار ينتظرون السماح لهم بالدخول.
تجولت فى ممرات المدرسة والتى لم يكتمل بناء طابقها
الثانى بسبب منع سلطات الاحتلال توسيعها ... وقعت
عينى على ملصق كبير معلق على واجهة الممر يقول:«
من حقى أن أتعلم وأعيش بكرامة» .. تسمّرت أمام هذه
العبارة أقرؤها المرة تلو الأخرى... ولكنى عاجزة عن
تفسير المفارقات . وبدت روحى تنسلخ عن جسدى غربة
واغترابا.

آمنة زيد الكيلانى.

لقد سمعنا عن العديد من المشاكل التى واجهتها النساء على الحواجز، كتلك الطبية التى تمت تعريتها وتفتيشها على الحاجز، أخريات تم احتجازهن على الحواجز، محاضرة من جامعة القدس وتسكن فى مدينة القدس حدثتنا عن تجربتها عندما توجهت الى عملها فى جامعة القدس فى ابوديس وفى طريق العودة اكتشفت أنها نسيت بطاقة هويتها فى البيت، لم يسمح لها بالمرور عبر الحاجز، واضطرت للانتظار هناك لمدة طويلة حتى قدم والدها الى الحاجز ومعه بطاقة هويتها لتتمكن فى النهاية من الوصول الى بيتها.

لذلك وللنساء اللاتى لديهن عائلات لا يفضل أن يعملن فى الجهة الأخرى من الحاجز العسكرى لأنها مخاطرة كبيرة لهن.

زائرة الى فلسطين مع مشروع قصص من أمهاتنا
(بريطانيا)

يوم الثلاثاء السادس عشر من كانون الأول عام ألفين وثلاثة.. لم يكن يوماً عادياً لإنسان عادى مثلى.... توقفت وأسرتى المكونة من زوجى وابنى وابنتى على مدخل جدار الفصل العنصرى على بوابة حديدية الكترونية وسط جمع من الجنود المدججين بالسلاح والسترات الواقية...

بالأمس القريب كانت قرية أم الريحان التى أسكنها، قرية جميلة وادعة تحتضنها أيكة خضراء... تسعد الناظر... واليوم أصبحت حبيسة وأبناؤها أصبحوا داخل معتقل كبير يتحركون رهن إشارة .. جندى أرعن .. استجلب من بلاد الشرق أو الغرب...

كنا فى ذلك اليوم نودع قريتنا... فى طريقنا إلى مركز عملنا ... فى مديريات التربية والتعليم فى كل من جنين وقباطية .... عندما طلب الجنود منا التوقف نحن وبقية المواطنين ... وعدم الاقتراب منهم أو اختراق البوابة الحديدية ... توقف الجميع .. رجال ونساء... موظفون .. عمال ... طلبة مدارس صغار يحملون حقائبهم المدرسية...

رتّب الجميع أنفسهم بين راجل وراكب، وبدأ العد التنازلى بالإشارة من الجندى بالتحرك نحوه.. كان على الرجال رفع ملابسهم العلوية.. والاستدارة بشكل دائرى على بعد أمتار من الجندى... ثم الاقتراب والتدقيق فى البطاقات فرداً فرداً.. أما المرحلة الثالثة من مراحل الذل والهوان فتتمثل بتهديدهم بضرورة الحصول على تصريح للخروج والعودة إلى بيوتهم.

لم تسلم براءة الأطفال من نازية القرن الحادى والعشرين .. عندما استدعى أطفال متوقفون على البوابة بضرورة الانتظام

فى طابور وفتح حقائبهم المدرسية .. لم يرتبك الأطفال .. ولم يبدوا أى وجل أو خوف.. تقدموا الواحد تلو الآخر... والجندى يشير بضرورة فتح الحقائب ... يخرج الأطفال دفاترهم الرسم وبقايا أقلامهم الصغيرة ... وأشياءهم الخاصة ويعيدون ترتيبها مرة ثانية وسط فوهات البنادق المصوبة نحوهم ويسيرون إلى مدرستهم القريبة (فى قرية طورة) سيراً على الأقدام متسللين عبر أشجار الزيتون القائمة وتلك التى اقتلعتها الجرافات من جذورها لبناء الجدار اللعين .

استدعيت وأفراد أسرتى للمثول أمام الجندى ..توقفت محركات السيارة .. وطلب منا النزول جميعاً وتم التدقيق فى بطاقاتنا ... كانت الساعة تراوح الثامنة صباحاً.. عندما جاء دورى فى الفحص والتفتيش .. لم يكتف الجندى بالبطاقة الشخصية .. بل طلب منى فتح حقيبتى الشخصية وملفات الأوراق التى بحوزتى .. كنت أنظر إليه باحتقار شديد ... فلم أعهد جنوداً بهذه الشراسة وانعدام الإنسانية .

أشار إلىّ وابنتى التى ترافقنى أن أذهب إلى خيمة صغيرة قد نصبت على مقربة من البوابة بحجة تفتيش النساء .. لم أنصع للأمر... لأنى وجدت فى ذلك إهانة لكرامتى وإنسانيتى وعروبتى .. وانتهاكاً لحقوقى وأنا تلك التى عملت فى التدريس عشرين سنة.. أزرع القيم والمبادئ الإنسانية المتمثلة فى الدفاع عن الحق والكرامة فى الأجيال جيلاً بعد جيل .. لم أحتمل هول ما جرى .. ليس خوفاً أو جبناً وإنما حفاظاً على حقى وحق ابنتى فى أن تصان كرامتنا...

Work

Tuesday sixteenth of December 2003 was not a normal day for an ordinary person like me. I was stopped with my family, husband, son and daughter, at the entrance of the Racist Separation Wall at the iron electronic gate amidst a group of heavily armed soldiers wearing bulletproof vests.

Not long ago, the village of Um al-Reehan, where I live, was a beautiful, tranquil place hugged by a lush green wood, a pleasant scene. Today it has become a besieged place and its inhabitants are prisoners who follow the orders of impatient foreign soldiers.

That day we left our village on our way to work in the Education Directorates in Jenin and Qabatyah. The soldiers asked us and other people to stop and not to approach them or to pass through the iron gate. All of us stopped: men, women, office workers, labourers and small school children carrying their school bags. We arranged ourselves: passengers in one line and motorists in another. The countdown started. At a signal from a soldier, men had to lift up their upper clothes and to turn in a circle a few meters from the soldier. Following that, they were asked to move one by one for meticulous inspection of their IDs. Then a third stage of humiliation and insults, and a threat that they would need travel permits to leave or return to their homes.

Even small children did not escape the cruelty of the Nazis of the twenty-first century. They were told to stand in a queue and to open their school bags. The children did not look bothered, afraid or worried. One after the other, they were ordered by the soldier to open their bags, and they stepped forward. Out came their drawing notebooks, whatever was left of their short pencils and other objects. They repacked their bags with the soldiers' guns directed at them, and walked to their school in Tourah village across fields of olive trees, some of which were uprooted by bulldozers to build the cursed Wall.

I was called with my family to stand before the soldier. The engine of the car was switched off and a soldier told us to get out. This was about eight o'clock in the morning. The soldier was not satisfied with inspecting my ID but asked me to open my hand bag and the files I had with me. I looked at him with great contempt: I have never experienced such cruel soldiers. They had lost their humanity and had no respect for my right or the right of my daughter to our dignity.

The soldier ordered me and my daughter to go to a small tent put up near the gate for the inspection of women. I refused to obey the order because I found it insulting and humiliating and a violation of my human rights to do so. I worked for twenty years as a teacher cultivating human values, dignity and human rights in generation after generation. How could I take this from a soldier?

My husband and son were standing near the 'tent of humiliation' when I started screaming at the soldiers to leave us alone and not to come near us. The soldiers' response was sudden and quick; we would not be allowed to get out or pass through the gate. They then threatened my husband with beating and arrest if we did not go back to where we came from. We were obliged but it was horrible, our blood boiling with anger and pain. All exits were now shut before us.

My daughter cried because she was deprived of her natural right to go to school. We were all silent not knowing what to do. I did not go immediately to my house but I instead I visited the village school to carry out some observation work.

Some children were in the school yard waiting for their teachers who were at the other side of the wall to be allowed to pass through the gate. I walked through the corridors of the school whose second floor was not finished; the occupation authorities prevented its completion. My sight fell on a big poster put up in one of the corridors reading "IT IS MY RIGHT TO LEARN AND TO LIVE WITH DIGNITY". I froze before this phrase reading it time and again but unable to explain the contradictions. My soul seemed to break away from my body. I felt alienated and subdued.

Aminah Zaid Alkilani

I heard many stories about women's problems getting to work. Women from Abu Dis with West Bank IDs were not able to go on working in Jerusalem. Some of them used to be teachers in Jerusalem schools. When they started building the Separation Wall, first they walked round it, later they used to jump over low parts of it, but now they can't go there so they have lost that work.

We heard about terrible problems at checkpoints. A woman doctor was stopped and strip searched. Others are held up. A woman lecturer who lives in Jerusalem told us that one day she went to work in the university in Abu Dis but she forgot her ID. She wasn't allowed to go home for a long time. she had to wait in the checkpoint until her father found her ID and came and brought it to the checkpoint so she could go home.

So for women with families in particular it means it is a real risk to work on the other side of a checkpoint.

British visitor to Palestine with the Stories from our Mothers project

ولادة

هذة سندس وابنتها لميس، اذا لم تكونوا تعرفوا، فلميس ولدت على حاجز.

لم تستطع الوصول الى المستشفى فى طولكرم بسبب الحواجز.

هناك حاجزا تفتيش إسرائيليين تحيطنا ببيت ليد حاجز عناب وحاجز الكفريات لا يمكن أن نعبر الى مدينة طولكرم دون أن نمر على احد الحاجزين، حاجز عناب يغلق فى الساعة الخامسة، فى بداية الانتفاضة لا احد كان يستطيع المرور بعد الساعة الخامسة لذلك سلكنا الطريق الآخر الى نقطة التفتيش كفرات.

أخبرت سيارة الإسعاف أن تأتى وتأخذها من بيت ليد لأنها بحاجه الى أن تصل المستشفى للولادة قالت له (تعال الى الحاجز سأنتظرك فى الجانب الآخر للحاجز) ولكن سيارة الإسعاف لم تستطع الوصول إليها.

قالت للجندى على الحاجز أنها تحتاج للمرور عبر الحاجز لأنها تريد أن تضع مولودا وتحتاج للذهاب الى المستشفى،

فرد الجندى (انه ليس لدى أوامر للسماح لك بالمرور، يمكنك البقاء هنا حتى نحصل على الأوامر لتركك تمرين).

بدأت هى وأمها بالبكاء، زوجها سأل الجندى (هل هناك طبيب على الحاجز ليساعد زوجتى هى تحتاج الى طبيب ومستشفى فأجاب لا يوجد طبيب).

بعد ذلك أنجبت طفلتها فى السيارة، زوجها والسائق كانوا خارج السيارة لأنهم يتكلمون مع الجنود كانوا يحاولون إقناع الجندى بضرورة السماح لهم بالمرور الى المستشفى وحين عاد زوجها والسائق الى السيارة شاهدوا الطفل.

كانت خائفة جدا لأن الطفل يحتاج الى العناية الطبية بعد ذلك سمح الجنود لها بالمرور، وصلت فى النهاية مع طفلتها الى المستشفى.

وصفية عثمان

Giving birth

These are Sundus and her daughter Lamees. Do you know, Lamees was born at a checkpoint. Sundus couldn't get to the hospital in Tulkarem because of the checkpoints.

There are two checkpoints around Beit Leed village – Anat and Kafreat. If we go to Tulkarem, or to Jenin or Nablus, we have to go past one of these checkpoints.

Since the beginning of the intifada, Anat checkpoint has been closed at 5 o'clock: nobody can pass after 5 o'clock. So when she started to go into labour in the evening, Sundus took the other road to Kafreat checkpoint.

She told the ambulance; "You can come to take me from Beit Leed. Come to the checkpoint and I'll wait for you on the other side". She went to the checkpoint but the ambulance couldn't reach her.

She told the soldier that she needed to go through the checkpoint because she needed to give birth in a hospital. But he told her, "We don't have an order from the officer to let you pass the checkpoint, You can stay here until we have the order saying that you can go through."

She began to cry and her mother as well. Her husband asked the soldier, "Do you have a doctor here to help my wife? She needs a doctor and a hospital." He was told, "No no".

After that, she gave birth to the baby in the car. Her husband and the driver were outside the car because they were talking to the soldiers, still trying to persuade them to let them take her through to the hospital. And they came back to the car and saw the baby.

She was very afraid because the baby needed medical care in the hospital. But then, when the baby was born, they allowed her to pass and she and she and the baby reached the hospital.

Wasfia Othman

129

امومه

ولدت فى نابلس فى قرية اسمها عوريف الى الجنوب من نابلس عمرى 21 عام ولكن لصعوبة ما مررت به من تجربة قاصية اشعر أننى فى الخمسين من العمر. أنا سيدة متزوجة وعندى طفل حديث الولادة وأنا طالبة فى كلية الصيدلة فيجامعة النجاح فى نابلس.

توفي ابنى الاول فى السنة الاولى من الانتفاضة، قبل أن أتزوج لم أكن اعرف شىء عن الحياة، تزوجت وسجلت فى جامعة النجاح وبعد ذلك بدأت الانتفاضة، فكرت فى ترك الجامعة ولكن مع التشجيع الذى لاقيته من عائلتى دفعنى لإكمل تعليمى.

الطريق الى نابلس من بلدتى أصبح ملىء بالمعاناة، كنت حامل وكنت كل الوقت قلقة جدا على صحة الجنين وكذلك قلقة على زوجى الذى فقد عمله ويقيم كل الوقت فى البيت بانتظار عودتى، أنا سيدة ريفية وقد أصبح موقفى جدا حرج فى قريتى فكيف اخرج كل يوم وأعود الى القرية فى المساء؟

تعمد الجنود الإسرائيليون تأخيرنا كل يوم على الحواجز فى بعض الأحيان كنا نمضى ساعات فى الانتظار، تقريبا كنت أنا السيدة الوحيدة فى الحافلة مما يشعرنى كل الوقت بالإحراج ولكن لم يكن أمامى خيار كان لابد من أن أكمل تعليمى.

عندما أنجبت الطفل الاول، كان ضعيفاً جداً من جراء الضغط الذى تعرضت أنا له خلال فترة الحمل. ذهبت الى الطبيب الذى قال انه يتوجب نقل الطفل الى المستشفى قال(أن حالة الطفل حرجة ويتوجب نقله الى المستشفى بإمكانكم استخدام سيارتى).

لم يسمح الجنود المتواجدين على الحاجز لنا بالتنقل بالسيارة وقد انتظرنا لأكثر من ثلاث ساعات قبل أن تصل سيارة إسعاف وكان الجو حارا جدا.

عند وصولنا الى المستشفى، سألونى لماذا تأخرت بالطفل لقد كان طفلى ضعيفا جدا وقد توفى.
من الواضح أن الجنود الإسرائيليون قتلوا طفلى.

الى متى ستستمر معاناتنا، ننجب أطفال ونربيهم ونكبرهم ونحافظ عليهم حتى نراهم يقتلون بدم بارد.

هذة قصة فلسطينية روتها فيحاء عبد الهادى فى ورشة العمل لمشروع قصص من أمهاتنا فى جامعة القدس، كانت تحاول تسليط الضوء على العبء المضاعف الذى يقع على المرأة فى فلسطين الضغط الاجتماعى والاقتصادى وبالإضافة الى أعباء الاحتلال الإسرائيلى، ووضحت هيفاء انه رغم كل الضغوط فان المرأة ازدادت قوة وعزيمة.

130

Motherhood

I was born in Nablus, I am 21 years old but my experience has made me more like 50 years old. I am a married woman with a newborn baby. I am a student of chemistry at An Najah University in Nablus.

My first baby died during the first years of the Intifada. Before I was married, I knew nothing of life. I got married and registered at the University. After that, the Intifada started. I thought of leaving university, but with my family's encouragement, I continued my education.

The road to Nablus from my village became full of suffering. I was pregnant and afraid for the health of my unborn baby and aware of my husband who stayed at home and waited for my return. I'm a village woman and my position in the village became very sensitive: how could I come home late?

The Israeli soldiers started to delay us, sometimes for hours. I was often the only woman in the taxi and it was very embarrassing, sometimes unbearable.

But I had to continue my study.

When the baby was born, it was weak because of all the pressures we had gone through. I went to the doctor who said that the baby had to go to hospital. He said, "It is urgent – take my car"; but the soldiers would not let us through the checkpoint. We had to wait three hours in the extreme summer heat.

When we got to the hospital, they asked me why I had delayed – my baby was very weak, and finally he died.

It seems that the soldiers made death my child's fate.

How long will we live this suffering, giving birth to children, bringing them up, guarding over them, and watching them being killed in cold blood?

This account by a Palestinian woman was one of the stories told by Faiha Abulhadi during the Stories from our Mothers workshop at the Al Quds University. She was trying to highlight the many sorts of pressures that confront Palestinian women: Faiha explained how all these pressures – social and economic as well as pressures coming from the Israeli Occupation – are making Palestinian woman stronger and more determined.

الصحة وكبار السن

تحملت أنا وزوجي المفاجأة وصبرنا على ذلك، وأصبح يتردد على العلاج كل أسبوع وذات يوم ذهبنا لأخذ وجبة العلاج الكيماوى لزوجى فى المطلع ومررنا عن الحاجز القريب من المنزل للخروج الى المستشفى فى القدس من الساعة الثامنة صباحا وعدنا الى البيت الساعة الخامسة مساءً.

بعد ثلاث ساعات من عودتنا تعب زوجى حيث صار يلهث ويتنفس بسرعة أخذناه الى أقرب مركز صحى (كوبات حوليم) وهناك كان يجب أن ندفع مصاريف علاجه لأنه من الضفة حيث قدموا له الإسعاف الأولى ولكن بعدها توفى زوجى رحمة الله.

حضرت سيارة الإسعاف لنقل جثمانه الى مستشفى المقاصد ولكن الحاجز العسكرى رفض السماح لسيارة الإسعاف الدخول الى مدينة القدس لأن من تحمله ميت سألتهم لماذا؟ قالوا لى لأنه توفى وبذلك انتهت إقامته وتصريحه، بعد ذلك قررنا نقل الجثمان الى مدينة الخليل عن طريق واد النار التى هى طريق يسمح لحملة هوية الضفة الغربية فقط المرور بها، لم يسمح الجنود لى بالمرور عبر حاجز (الكنتينر) لأنى أحمل هوية القدس ومنعت من الدخول مع زوجى أيضا وهذا من أبسط حقوقى كأرملة أن ارافق جثمان زوجى وأن أحضر مراسم دفنه.
هذة قصتى ومعاناتى مع الهوية.

ليلى الشريف

أنا سيدة من القدس وأسكن فيها أحمل الهوية الزرقاء المقدسية وزوجى يحمل الهوية الخضراء هوية الضفة الغربية قدمت لزوجى جمع شمل من أجل المكوث عندى فى القدس وكان ذلك سنة 1995.

مرت سنين عدة ولم يستطيع زوجى أخذ الهوية المقدسية، مرض زوجى وقدمت له تصريح ومعاملة للعلاج فى مستشفى المقاصد والمطلع فى القدس أخذنا التصريح والمعاملة للعلاج وبعدها تبين انه مريض بسرطان الرئة.

132

Ill health and old age

I'm a woman from Jerusalem and I have a blue Jerusalem ID. My husband had a green West Bank ID. In 1995, I applied for a "family reunion" – permission for my husband to come and live with us in Jerusalem.

Years passed by, and my husband did not manage to have a Jerusalem ID. After some time, he got ill. I applied for permission for him to have treatment at Al Muqassed and Augusta Victoria hospitals in Jerusalem. We got the permission, and he managed to pass through. And we discovered that he had cancer of the kidney.

My husband and I managed to cope with the shock and my husband started to go to the hospital for treatment each week.

One day, when we went with my husband to have chemotherapy as usual, we passed through the checkpoint, near our house, to go to the hospital in Jerusalem. We had to stay at the hospital from 8 in the morning till 5 in the afternoon, and then we returned to the refugee camp.

After three hours, my husband was really not well, and we decided to take him to the Kobat Kolim health centre. We paid for this because he was from the West Bank and it is forbidden for him to have treatment under Israeli health insurance. There, they gave him first aid, but inside the health centre, he died, God rest his soul.

After that an ambulance came to take him to the Al Muqassed hospital. But when we got to the military checkpoint, they would not let the ambulance through because it held a dead body. When I asked them why they wouldn't let him go through, they said, "He is dead and his permission to travel has expired, so he can't go through the checkpoint."

We decided to take him to bury him in Hebron. But the ambulance needed to go through the Container Checkpoint in Wad al-Nar. This road is meant to be just for West Bankers. So I am not allowed to go on that road because I have a blue ID.

So I was not allowed to go with him. It is my right as a widow to go to my husband's funeral, but I was not allowed to go.

Layla Sharif

ليست النهاية

هذا حقا محزن جدا أن الغرب لم يستطع فهم هذا، الغربيون يخلطون الأمور، ونحن من جانبنا نرفض أدعائهم بأنه لا يوجد في مجتمعنا ديمقراطية، لأن ديمقراطيتنا وحريتنا تسحق تحت أقدام الإسرائيليين ، أين حقوق الانسان خاصتنا ؟

كان الإعلان العالمي لحقوق الانسان مثير جدا، يجب علينا جميعاً احترام حقوق الانسان ، ولكن حقوق الانسان الفلسطيني لا تحترم، ونحن لا نعامل حتى كآدميين، ولا يحرك الغرب ساكن فهم فقط يراقبون، القليل منهم يرفض ذلك والقليل يعترض والقليل يفعل شيء.

نحن نعول على الجماهير فهم يقدرون على التغيير انتم من يصوت وينتخب الساسة والقادة.

لا نريد منكم أن تعملوا لنا كفلسطينيين، اعملوا لمستقبل أطفالكم، كيف تستطيع أن تخطط للسلام العالمي والتوافق والأمن، بدون إنهاء كل المعاناة التي يتعرض لها الفلسطينيين والتي ستؤثر بالطبيعي على كل أرجاء العالم وصولاً الى أمريكا وأوروبا.

صدقوني، نحن نهتم كثيرا، نهتم، ونعرف ما معنى الاستفزاز وما معنى الذل اليومي، صدقوني، أنا من القدس وأبي كان رئيس بلدية القدس لسبع سنوات، وأنا الآن لا استطيع زيارة القدس منذ عشر سنوات، الآن حياتنا تقرر من قبل الإسرائيليون، سواء بقينا هنا أو ذهبنا الى الخارج يملكون القوة ويستطيعون إثبات ما يريدون.

ما نطالبكم به هو أن تأخذوا مواقف مبدئية، لا تقفوا في صفنا، ضعوا أنفسك مكاننا وتصرفوا على هذا الأساس.
ماذا تتوقعون أن يكون شعور الفلسطينيين؟ أنظروا الى الهجوم الموجه الآن ضد أهل القدس، يطردهم الإسرائيليون من بيوتهم، ويعيشون خارج بيوتهم داخل الخيام وكل بضعة أيام يأتون ويدمرون الخيام....

كيف تتوقعون أن يكون شعور الفلسطينيين؟ يريدون إخراجهم من مدينتهم، لقد كذبوا لمدة أربعين سنةً بأن الفلسطينيين اختاروا ترك بلادهم ولم يجبرهم أحد على ذلك، وقد كشف (آلين بابيه) الذي نشر وثائق وبراهين دامغة بان قرار التهجير كان إسرائيلياً، هم من أخرجوا المواطنين الفلسطينيين من بيوتهم ولم يكن القرار فقط بإخراج الناس بل بأن تدمر كل قراهم ومنازلهم وأن لا يترك حجراً على آخر في القرى الفلسطينية حتى لا يفكر أحد يوما ما في العودة.

هذا ما نشعر به وهذا خبزنا اليومي وجبيننا اليومي ومعاناتنا اليومية ما الذي يفعله الإسرائيليون بنا.

دعونا نوقف هذا الغضب بإيجاد مناخ من العدالة والمساواة واحترام حقوق الانسان.

أنا ولدت في بئر السبع وهي الآن مدينة إسرائيلية، في هويتي الشخصية مكتوب مكان الولادة بئر السبع، قبل أيام سألني شخص هل أنت إسرائيلية؟ لقد كان سعيدا .. أنا أجبته: (لا، لكن أنا ولدت قبل أن تولد دولتكم).

هذا جزء من معاناتنا، جزء بسيط، وأتمنى أن تساعدني لغتي الانجليزية لأخبركم بأكثر وأكثر. هذا جزء مما نشعر به، ونحن حقا نطالب بريطانيا - بشكل رئيسي - لتعديل وعد بلفور الذي كان بداية لمعاناتنا وبداية بؤسنا في فلسطين، أعطى قادتكم وعدا لليهود وهم لا زالوا يدعمون إسرائيل بكل شيء، والآن انتم تحملون المسؤولية.

نحن لا نريد إبادة الإسرائيليين ولا نريد أن نرمي أحدا بالبحر هم يرمونا، لكن أتيحوا لنا المجال كي نعيش واتركوهم يعيشون.

من الحديث مع الزوار البريطانيين من قبل فريدة العمد مديرة جمعية إنعاش الأسرة رام الله

136

لو كنتم مكاننا

يترددون للحظة فى مساندة إسرائيل، لأنهم بداية صدقوا الأكاذيب التى ينتجها الإسرائيليون عندما يدعون (أن هذه بلادهم والفلسطينيون لا يملكون أى حق فيها) وثانيا لان الإسرائيليون نجحوا فى ابتزاز الغرب.

لكن على مدار أربعة عشر عاماً من المفاوضات لم نصل الى أى نتيجة، لن يكون الإسرائيليون أبداً جاهزون لإرجاع أى مما سلبوه، قلنا نحن جاهزون بأن نعود للمفاوضات على أن توقف إسرائيل البناء وتوسيع المستوطنات وإلا فما فائدة المفاوضات.

لكن على مدار أربعة عشر عاماً من المفاوضات لم نصل الى أى نتيجة، لن يكون الإسرائيليون أبداً جاهزون لإرجاع أى مما سلبوه، قلنا نحن جاهزون بأن نعود للمفاوضات على أن توقف إسرائيل البناء وتوسيع المستوطنات وإلا فيما فائدة المفاوضات.

هذا ليس شأناً دينياً نحن كان لدينا أصدقاء من اليهود وكنا نذهب الى أعيادهم وكانوا يأتون ويزوروننا فى أعيادنا ونفس الشىء أيضا مع المسيحيون كلنا عشنا بتوافق.

نحن فى فلسطين نفخر باحترام كل الأديان ونحن نحترم كل الأديان، لكن نرفض الاستعمار ونرفض الاحتلال، نرفض من يذلنا ويهيننا يوميا على الحواجز.

شكلنا لجنة للاعتناء بتراثنا وثقافتنا. مهمة هذه اللجنة جمع ونشر وعمل كل ما يمكن من اجل الحفاظ على ثقافتنا وتراثنا ونقلها من جيل الى آخر، لان ما نواجهه من الإسرائيليين خطير جدا، فشغلهم الشاغل منذ بداية الاحتلال كان محو كل ما هو فلسطينى.

للأسف فإن الغرب إنحاز وبشكل أعمى لجانب الاحتلال متجاهلين الظلم الذى يقع علينا، الى حد أن إسرائيل أضحت الطفل المدلل للغرب، بشكل رئيسى لأمريكا مع التبعية المطلقة من قبل الأوروبيين والبريطانيين الذين لا

In our shoes

We started a committee to look after our heritage and culture. The job of this committee is to collect, to publish, to do everything possible to get our culture and heritage to go from one generation to another. Because what we are facing from the Israelis is very, very dangerous. It has been their job since they occupied Palestine to erase everything that is Palestinian.

Unfortunately our struggle with the Israelis has been supported blindly by the West, to the extent that Israel has become the pampered child of the West, mainly of America but then Europe and Britain follows suit, they don't hesitate a minute, because first of all they bought the Israelis' big lies when they said, "This is our country and the Palestinians have no right in it"; and secondly because they are blackmailed.

Many of you have experienced occupation when Hitler was there. I have not heard of a country that did not reject occupation – people reject occupation – here, with the most basic of resources, against a country which has the fifth biggest army in the world.

We said "Let them live and let us live, we are not asking for much, we are just asking for implementation of United Nations resolutions to have an end to this struggle." We thought the whole world would support us with our quest for peace – it is very painful to get rid of half your country for the sake of peace, but since 14 years we got nowhere. The Israelis are never ready to give back anything. We say, "We are ready to negotiate, but stop settlements and settlement enlargement,or what is the use of negotiations?"

This is not about religion. We used to have friends who were Jews, we used to go to their feasts, they used to come and visit us on our feasts. It was the same with Christians, we all lived in harmony. We in Palestine were proud to admire all religions and we respect all religions. But we reject colonialism, we reject occupation, we reject somebody humiliating us daily at the checkpoints.

It is really very sad that the West does not understand this, they mix things together. Don't let them tell us they are trying to sell us democracy when our democracy is being crushed under the feet of the Israelis.

Where are our human rights? The declaration of human rights was very exciting. We should all respect human rights – but our human rights are not respected and we are not even treated as humans – and this with all the West just watching. Very few are rejecting, very few are objecting, very few are doing something.

We rely on people: only people can change the facts on the ground. You elect your leaders...

Don't work for us as Palestinians. Work for the future of your children. How can you plan for a world of peace, harmony, security, if there is injustice? How can we? If we want to live in peace, all of us? And what is happening here is going to affect each and everybody in all the world, Europe and America.

And believe me, we care very much, we care. We know what it is to be harassed. We know how bitter it is to be humiliated daily. Believe me, I am from Jerusalem and my father was the Mayor of Jerusalem for seven years, and now I have been prohibited from even visiting Jerusalem for ten years. Now our life is decided by the Israelis: whether we should live here, go outside, whatever. They have the power, they impose anything.

Now you should stand for principles, don't stand for us. Put yourself in our shoes and act accordingly.

What do they expect the Palestinians to feel? Look at the attack now on people from Jerusalem. The Israelis are kicking people out and they have to stay in tents, and every few days the Israelis come and demolish the tents. How can you expect the Palestinians to feel? The Israelis want them out! They lied for forty years that Palestinians chose to leave their country, that no one forced them to leave. Now Ilan Pappe comes with documents, with proof that it was an Israeli decision, and the decision was not only to throw the people out, but not to leave a stone in that village, so that they can never come back again.

This is how we feel, this is our daily bread and butter and our daily suffering, what the Israelis are doing to us.

Let's stop this anger from building, through justice, through equality, through respecting people's rights.

I was born in Beersheeba, now an Israeli city. But on my ID is written 'Place of birth: Beersheeba'. The other day someone asked me "Are you Israeli?" He was happy. I said "No, but I was born before your state was born."

So these are some of the things we are suffering – just some – I couldn't express – I wish my English could help me to tell you more and more and more. This is part of what we feel.

And we really ask Britain – mainly – to rectify their Balfour Declaration which was the start of our agony and the start of our misery in Palestine. They gave the Israelis the right, and they supported them. And now you carry the responsibility.

We don't want to annihilate the Israelis – we don't want to throw anybody in the sea – they are throwing us – but let them live and let us live.

From a talk to the British visitors by Farida Alamad, Director of In'ash al Usra, Ramallah

139

إفعلوا شيئاً

النكبة..... هل تبدو هذه الكلمة مألوفة لديكم؟ تعني الكارثة، تعني المأساة، وعام 1948 كان بالنسبة لنا بمثابة مأساة.

جيد أنكم أتيتم الى القدس اليوم لتروا بأعينكم الأمور الرهيبة التي تحدث في القدس الشرقية.

منذ طفولتي كنا نخرج الى الشوارع لنتظاهر ضد وعد بلفورد، والآن توقفت، ليس لأني كبرت في السن، لكن لأنه عندما تقع الأحداث على غرار ما فعلت هيلاري كلينتون البارحة، في وقوفها بجانب نتنياهو وموافقتها على كل ما يريده..... وعندما قالت، (عودوا الى المفاوضات) **أتساءل ماذا بقى للتفاوض عليه؟؟ انسى الأمر...... انسيه.**

الساسة يعرفون جيداً حقيقة ما يحدث، ويعلمون انه لا يمكن فعل أي شيء لإيقافه، فهذا حديث المال، وأعضاء الكونجرس الأمريكي جل طموحهم أن يتم انتخابهم مرة أخرى.

(سؤال من سيدة بريطانية) لقد اظهرتي غضبك وخيبت املك مما يحدث، اخبرينا ماذا تريدى منا أن نفعل؟

حسناً، على اعتبار أننا نلتقى اليوم 2 تشرين ثاني ذكرى وعد بلفورد المشئوم، فأملنا بكم أن تقروا جيداً ما حدث، عندما يقوم شخص بإعطاء اليهود الحق في أن يبنوا وطنهم في فلسطين ..... فهل هذا صواب؟ على أى أساس أعطى هذا الوعد؟

من الممكن أن تشكلوا مجموعة تسمى زيارة بلفورد؟ أن تشكلوا مجموعة لإعادة دراسة وعد بلفورد، الألم الذى سببه هذا الوعد لطرف، والهدية التى قدمها للطرف الآخر.

صحيح أن القصد كان بان تعطى جنة لليهود؟ اذا كان هذا صحيحاً، من الممكن أن تكون فلسطين جنة للناس على الأرض. في البداية اعتقدنا أنهم يبحثون عن ملاذ أمن، أصبح الناس هنا يوفرون لهم مساكن للإيجار في بناياتهم ويقدمون لهم المعونة، ولكن سرعان ما علمنا أنهم يريدون الأرض بدون السكان الأصليين.

اخبرني والدى أن القادمين الأوائل تم قبولهم كلاجئين ولكن بعد ذلك اتضح أننا لم نفهم الأمور كما هي، فالقصد كان بان يخلقوا دولة. لقد اتضحت الأمور أكثر في الأعوام 1947- 1948 وقد فهمنا أن هؤلاء الناس قادمين من اجل احتلال أرضنا وطرد سكانها.
هل مات بلفورد؟ البريطانيون لازالوا موجودين والحكومة البريطانية لازالت موجودة والشعب البريطاني كذلك. ويجب عليكم أن تفعلوا شيء بحق بلفورد.....

على كل الأحوال عاودوا زيارة وعد بلفورد، وشاهدوا ما يفعله بنا الآن. على كل البريطانيون أن يعملوا ضد وعد بلفورد.
نهلة العسلي

You should
do something

Jews a homeland in Palestine. You have to read the words… Who is right? What capacity did they have to make the promise?

So maybe you could make a group that is called

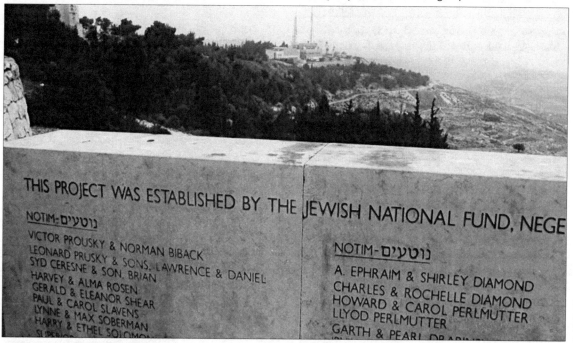

Nakba… is that word familiar to you? It means disaster, it means catastrophe. And 1948 for us was a catastrophe.

It is good that you come here and see the horrible things that are happening in East Jerusalem.

As kids we used to go out in the streets to demonstrate against the Balfour Declaration, now I gave up. Not because I'm old, but because it is futile. When things happen like what Hilary Clinton did yesterday, standing next to Netanyahu, agreeing to everything he wants. When she says "go back to negotiations" what is there to negotiate about? Forget it… forget it…

The politicians know what is happening, they know they cannot do anything, money speaks louder, and the Congress people want to be re-elected.

(Question from the British women) **You have been angry and you have been hopeless, but tell us, what do you want us to do?**

Well, since we met on 2nd November with the commemoration of a letter that decided our fate like this, when someone decided to promise to give the

Revisiting Balfour? Make a group that studies Balfour – what pain, what grief it caused to other people.

Is it true that the intention was to give a haven to the Jews? If so all right, Palestine can give a haven to people in the land. In the beginning we thought they were looking for a safe place, people allowed them to rent apartments in their buildings etc, but later it became clear that they wanted the land without the people.

My father told me that the early-comers were accepted as people seeking refuge but then it became clear that this was not the intention, the intention was to create a state. It was in 1947-48 that things became clear and we understood that people were coming to occupy the land and drive the people out.

Is Balfour dead? The British are still there, the government is there, the people are there. I think you should do something about Balfour…

Anyway, revisit the Balfour Declaration, and see what it is doing for us now. Just the British people should work on the Balfour Declaration.

Nahla Assali

141

العودة لبلفور

بعد أن قام المستوطنين بطردهم من البيت والاستيلاء عليه، وهم الآن يراقبون العائلة الفلسطينية من وراء نوافذ البيت.

سألنا أفراد العائلة الفلسطينية أين يناموا لأننا لم نشاهد حتى بطانية من الممكن أن تستخدم للنوم فى خيامهم، وعلمنا أنه للمرة الثالثة على التوالى قامت السلطات الإسرائيلية بمصادرة كل محتوياتهم، ولا يعرفون حتى الآن ما يمكن أن يستخدموه لستر أنفسهم والحصول على الدفء، الليلة الطقس بارد وماطر فى أبوديس والقدس.

لقد بكت العديد منا على الوضع الصعب الذى تواجهه هذه العائلة، وكان هناك عائلة فلسطينية أخرى تعيش نفس الظروف فى الشارع المقابل، فيما سلمت ضواحى بأكملها أوامر إخلاء عسكرية يتوجب على ساكنيها ترك منازلهم والتشرد بسبب السياسات الإسرائيلية.

كل من قابلناهم اليوم ذكرونا بالثانى من تشرين ثانى وهو الذكرى السنوية لوعد بلفور عام 1917 وحملوا الحكومة البريطانية مسئولية إنشاء دولة لليهود على أرض فلسطين. لقد نص وعد بلفور على أن لا يتخذ أى إجراء من شأنه أن يؤثر على الحقوق المدنية أو الدينية للقوميات غير اليهودية فى فلسطين. لكن آلام الفلسطينيين واضح جدا ومستمر وفى اتساع، ونحن نشعر بأنه حان الوقت لأن تتحمل بريطانيا مسئوليتها فى تضميد جروح الفلسطينيين وتخفيف معاناتهم.

رسالة للناشر جزء من رسالة الى صحيفة محلية فى كامدن كتبتها مجموعة من السيدات البريطانيات خلال زيارتهن لفلسطين:

عزيزى الناشر

نحن أعضاء من مجموعة نساء ذهبنا فى زيارة الى أبوديس وفلسطين نظمتها جمعية صداقة كامدن أبوديس، بعد يومين من زيارتنا الى فلسطين، نود أن نخبر الناس فى كامدن عن أمر مهم رأيناه خلال زيارتنا.

هذا الصباح وخلال تجولنا فى مدينة القدس، صادفنا مجموعة من النساء يقفن مقابل بيت يزينه العلم الإسرائيلى، فى وسط الحشد سيدة فلسطينية تحمل طفلها(شاهد الصورة) هذة السيدة تنتمى الى عائلة تسكن فى خيمة مقابل البيت المذكور

Revisiting Balfour

no sign even of blankets. We learned that for the third time since they had been displaced, the Israeli authority in Jerusalem had taken away all the things they had around them, and they did not know what they would use to keep them warm tonight. Tonight it is raining, windy and very cold in Abu Dis and Jerusalem.

Part of a letter to the local newspaper in Camden written by British women visitors to Palestine:

Dear sir

We're part of a group of visitors to Abu Dis, Palestine, organised by the Camden Abu Dis Friendship Association—and after two days in Palestine, we are moved to tell other people in Camden just one of the things that we have seen.

This morning on a visit to Jerusalem, we found a crowd of women around a brazier opposite a house decorated with an Israeli flag. In the middle was a Palestinian woman and her baby (see this picture) who are part of the family that have been living on the pavement opposite their old house—since they were kicked out of it by the Israeli settlers who watch them, seemingly unperturbed, from their window.

We asked them where they are sleeping as we could see

Many of us were moved to tears by what seemed exceptional hardship, but there is another Palestinian family in a similar position in the next street, and whole neighbourhoods have been given eviction orders and face dispossession because of Israeli policy.

Today everyone we met reminded us that the 2nd November is the anniversary of the Balfour Declaration (1917) and that Britain bears much of the responsibility for "the establishment in Palestine of a national home for the Jewish people." The Balfour Declaration also said that "nothing shall be done which may prejudice the civil and religious rights of … non-Jewish communities in Palestine", but it is very clear that the pain to the Palestinians is still continuing and spreading, and we feel it is time that Britain took responsibility for healing these wounds....

العمل معاً

لقد شعرت ألمهم ومدى إصرارهم على التغلب عليه وعدم الاستسلام له.

تعلمنا أن أحد أهم ادوارنا هو أن نستمع الى قصصهن بالشكل الذى يرتأين طرحها به وبالنظام الذى يرينه مناسب.

تعلمنا أن كلمات من قبيل (قوى) و (إيجابى) تستخدم كثيراً وهى مهمةٌ للغاية، خاصةً بوجود كل الضغوط النفسية التى ولدت صدمةً كبيرة لهن، وعليه فهن على الدوام يكررن (أنه يجب أن نتعايش مع الواقع).

تعلمنا كم ملهم التعامل مع النساء الفلسطينيات، كيف أن لديهن كل الحق فى الغضب من نكران العالم لحقوقهن، والإستراتيجيات التى إخذتها النساء الفلسطينيات فى سبيل كسر العزلة المفروضة عليهن. كم هن طاهيات مميزات ويتمتعن بمستوى عالى من الترابط والمودة التى هى سمة المجتمع الفلسطينى والتى نحن نفتقدها فى بريطانيا.

(ماذا تعلمتى منهم؟) لقد كانوا مدهشين، كل عائله تعرضت لحادث مروع، ومع ذلك فهم لا يظهرون الغضب، لكن أقوياء جداً ونبلاء، لقد كان الكرم الذى حظينا به اينما ذهبنا يشعرنا بالاحراج، لقد اظهرت النساء درجةً عاليةٍ فى تمالكهم لاعصابهم رغم الظروف الصعبة، كانوا فخورين جداً بوطنهم وثقافتهم.

لقد شعرت ألمهم ومدى إصرارهم على التغلب عليه او الاستسلام له.

لقد كانوا ودودين ودافئين، ومثقفين جداً على الصعيد السياسى بالمقارنه بالنساء فى بريطانيا.

نساء مختلفات جداً مع وجهات نظر مقنعةٍ للغاية، إجتماعيات، وفخورات بتراثهن ومحبات لوطنهن.

الى النساء الفلسطينيات، ماذا تعلمتن من النساء البريطانيات؟

كم كن متفهمات وصبورات ومستعدات للإستماع والعمل للمساعدة حتى وإن كن عشن فى واقع مختلف عن الواقع الذى تعودن عليه.

يحترمن الوقتِ، ويتحركن بسرعةٍ، نزيهات، وبسيطات جداً فى حياتهن.

يعملن كفريق واحد، كسبن إحترام الجميع، يحترمن المواعيد، ملتزمات، وصبورات، ويشعرن بالمسؤولية، وقلوبهن دافئات.

> أعتقد بأنه مهم جداً أن نستمر فى تشكيل روابط الصداقة، وأن نتذكر على الدوام معاناتهم ونضالهم، بعد أن رأيت كل شىء بعينى تولدت لدى الرغبة فى محاولة نقل ما شاهدت لجميع من حولى بيث

144

Working together

Palestinian women, what did you learn from the British women?

How understanding they were and patient to hear and help and understand everybody even if they were different from the way they are…

Respect for time, moving fast, honesty, transparency, simplicity in their home life.

To work as a team, to be responsible, disciplined, to be on time, to be committed.

They are patient, responsible, warm-hearted.

British women, what did you learn from the Palestinian women?

We learned that one of the most important roles for us as women is to LISTEN to women's stories from their own perspective wherever they are placed within the system.

We learned that words such as "strong" and "positive" are used a lot and are very important. However we also learned that this was at a psychological cost of repressing their traumas and "getting on with it".

We learned how inspirational Palestinian women are, how rightfully angry at the neglect of the world, the strategies they use to overcome their isolation. What great cooks they are and the love of community that we in Britain seem largely to have lost.

That they were incredible. Every family had some awful thing happening to them, but they showed no anger, but just very strong and noble character. The generosity we encountered everywhere was sometimes close to embarrassing. Their whole composure shows so much dignity and pride in their country and culture.

I felt their suffering and their determination to rise above it and to never give up.

They are progressive, warm, feisty and a lot more politicised than the average UK woman.

Many different women with very diverse points of view but in general strong community feeling, proud of their heritage and loving their land.

145

ماذا بعد

لقد اكتشفنا أنه توجد أشياء كثيرة نشترك فيها كنساء فلسطينيات وبريطانيات.

نريد أن نتحدى الواقع الذى خلفه وعد بلفور: فليس من حق بريطانيا أن تقرر ماذا يجرى فى فلسطين.

لقد اكتشفنا أنه توجد أشياء كثيرة نشترك كنساء فلسطينيات وبريطانيات.

نود أن نعمل من أجل رفع المعاناة التى أحدثها وعد بلفور وممارسات البريطانيون فى فلسطين والتى أدت الى معاناة كبيرة للمرأة الفلسطينية تحت الاحتلال الإسرائيلى.

نرغب فى أن نواصل الاتصال معاً على صعيد الأفراد والمؤسسات النسويه.

نود أن نعمل معاً من أجل رفع درجة الوعى لدى النساء فى بريطانيا حول واقع حقوق الانسان والانتهاكات التى تتعرض لها المرأة الفلسطينية.

نود أن ننظم رحلات نسويه مستقبلية بيننا وأن نطور معا برامج وفعاليات بين البلدين.

نود أن نطور ونعمم فكرة التوأمة والصداقة بين المواقع البريطانية والفلسطينية حتى يتمكن الناس فى البلدين من العمل سويا بشكل متساوى من أجل نصرت قضايا حقوق الانسان للمرأة الفلسطينية ولكل قطاعات الشعب الفلسطينى.

What next

From the Palestinian and British women together:

We have found how much we share as Palestinian and British women.

We want to maintain contact as individual women and women's organisations.

We want to organise further women's visits and develop a future programme of shared activities between the two countries.

We want to challenge the assumptions built into the Balfour Declaration: it isn't up to Britain to decide what happens in Palestine.

We want to work to heal the pain caused by the Balfour Declaration and Britain's actions in Palestine which led to the immense suffering of Palestinian women under the Israeli occupation.

We want to work together to raise the awareness of British women more widely about the human rights issues faced by Palestinian women.

We want to promote the idea of twinning and friendship links between different places in Palestine and Britain so that people from both places can work together in an equal way to promote human rights for women and for everybody.

المؤسسات التي شاركت في المشروع

Organisations that took part in the project

المؤسسات الفلسطينية

Palestinian organisations:

في أبوديس

In Abu Dis

دار الصداقة

Dar Assadaqa

مدرسة أبوديس الإعدادية المختلطة (وكالة الغوث)

Abu Dis Co-Educational School (UNWRA)

مركز السلام في العيزرية

Aizariyeh Peace Centre

روضة الأمل

Al Amal Nursery

المرفأ للصحة النفسية

Al Marfa Centre for Pyschological Health

مركز جمعية المقاصد الصحي

Al Muqassed Health Society

جمعية النهضة

Al Nahda Society

لجنة المرأة في الإتحاد العام للنقابات

General Federation of Trades Unions Women's Committee

مركز إنسان لدراسات الجندر جامعة القدس

Insan Centre for Gender Studies, Al Quds University

مدرسة جيل الأمل

Jeel al-Amal School

في ارجاء الضفة الغربية

Across the West Bank

جمعية النجدة لتنمية المرأة الفلسطينية

Al Najdeh Society for Palestinian Women

جمعية الريف النسائية الساوية

Ar Reef Women's Society, As Sawiya

الجمعية النسويه في بيت فوريك

Beit Fourik Women's Society

الجمعية النسويه في بيت ليد

Beit Leed Women's Society

مركز دارنا نابلس

Darna Centre, Nablus

جمعية سيدات الخليل

Hebron Women's Society

مركز جنين للثقافة والإبداع

Jenin Creative and Cultural Centre

مؤسسة منديلا

Mandela-Palestine Society

الإغاثة الطبية الفلسطينية

Palestinian Health Relief

برنامج الحق في التعليم جامعة النجاح

Right to Education Society, University of An Najah

مركز السرايا في القدس

Saraya Centre, Jerusalem

المركز النسوى في مخيم شعفاط

Shu'fat Camp Women's Centre

جمعية إنعاش الأسرة رام الله

Society of In'ash al Usra, Ramallah

لجان العمل النسائي في يتما

Yitma Women's Society

المؤسسات البريطانية

British organisations:

في كامدن

In Camden

جمعية صداقة كامدن ابوديس

Camden Abu Dis Friendship Association

مشروع كالثروب

Calthorpe Project

نقابات عمال كامدن

Camden Trades Council

المركز الاجتماعى كاستلهافين

Castlehaven Community Centre

مركز الجندر في جامعة سوس

Centre for Gender Studies, School of Oriental and African Studies

مركز آباء كورام

Coram Parents Centre

جلوبال جنيراشن

Global Generation

Kentish Town Community Centre	المركز الاجتماعى فى كنتش تاون
London School of Economics Palestine Society	الجالية الفلسطينية فى كلية لندن للاقتصاد
Marchmont St Community Centre	المركز الاجتماعى مارشمنت ستريت
Mary Ward Centre	مركز مارى وورد
SOAS Palestine Society	الجالية الفلسطينية فى جامعة سوس
Somers Town Community Centre	المركز الاجتماعى سمرز تاون
University College London Palestine Society	الجالية الفلسطينية فى كلية لندن الجامعية
University of Westminster Students' Union	اتحاد طلبة جامعة ويسمنستر

Across Britain
Community groups, university groups, women's groups in Bournemouth, Cardiff, Cambridge, Canterbury, Kensington and Chelsea, Norwich, Southampton, Westminster

فى أنحاء بريطانيا:
المجموعات وطلبة الجامعات والمؤسسات النسوية فى بورنموث، كاردف، كامبرج، كنترباري، نوريش كنجستون وتشيلسى، ساوث هامتون، ويست منستر

Twinning groups that took part in the project:

مجموعات التوأمة البريطانية الفلسطينية التى شاركت فى المشروع:

149

Main partners in the visits
Camden—Abu Dis
South-East London—Beit Fourik
Tower Hamlets—Jenin
Haringey—Aizariyeh

الشركاء الرئيسيين فى الزيارات
صداقة كامدن أبوديس
صداقة جنوب شرق لندن وبيت فوريك
صداقة تور همليت وجنين
صداقة هيرنجا والعيزرية

Other twinning groups involved
Bristol—Gaza City
Chesham—Al Khader
Exeter—Hebron
Hastings—Yitmah
Liverpool—Bil'in
Llanidloes—As Sawiya
Luton—Battir
Manchester—Nablus
Newcastle—Azzoun
Pendle—Beit Leed
Staffordshire University—Hebron Polytechnic
Sterling—Shu'fat Camp
Waltham Forest—Beit Lahiya
Watford—Salfeet
Worcester—Khan Younis

بالإضافة الى توأمات أخرى شاركت فى المشروع
صداقة بريستل ومدينة غزة
صداقة تشيشام والخضر
صداقة اجستر الخليل
صداقة هيوستن ويتما
صداقة ليفربول وبلعين
صداقة لاند لويس والساوية
صداقة لوتون وبتير
صداقة مانسيستر ونابلس
صداقة نيوكاسيل وعزون
صداقة بندل وبيت ليد
صداقة جامعة ستافوردشاير ومعهد البوليتكنك
صداقة
صداقة ولثام فوست وبيت لاهيه
واتفورد سلفيت
صداقة وورکستر وخان يونس

These groups are all part of the Britain-Palestine Twinning Network

كل هذة المجموعات هى ضمن شبكة التوأمة البريطانية الفلسطينية

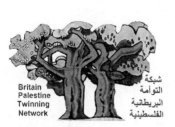

150

Lightning Source UK Ltd.
Milton Keynes UK
16 September 2010
159910UK00001B/20/P